Journal of a Horse Gunner
India to the Baltic via Alamein

The Author

Journal of a Horse Gunner
India to the Baltic via Alamein

by

Brigadier R. B. T. Daniell, DSO

Buckland Publications Ltd.
Chaucer House, Chaucer Business Park,
Kemsing, Sevenoaks, Kent TN15 6PW

Copyright © 1998 by the estate of the late Robert Bramston Thesiger Daniell
First Published 1998

This book is copyrighted under the Berne Convention. No portion may be reproduced by any process without the copyright holder's written permission except for the purposes of reviewing or criticism, as permitted under the Copyright Act of 1956.

ISBN 0 7212 0951 3

Printed and bound in Great Britain by
Buckland Press Ltd., Dover, Kent.

This book is for Betty, my much loved wife, who shared
with me every day of the last fifty-four years of my memoirs,
and is dedicated to all those gallant men
whom I had the honour to lead in battle.

My grateful thanks to Mrs Heather Spencer,
without whose generous help
this book could never have been written.

R.B.T.D.
October, 1983

CONTENTS

		Page
Foreword		11

Chapter
1	The Boy – 1912-1920	13
2	The Soldier	20
3	India	27
4	Secunderabad	39
5	The Equitation School, Saugor	48
6	The Masai Reserve, Tanganyika	53
7	Returning to India	63
8	Back in England	70
9	Palestine	82
10	The Western Desert Campaign	86
11	The Ten-month Siege of Tobruk and the Battle of the Cauldron	91
12	Retreat	99
13	The Turn of the Tide	104
14	Invasion Preparations	112
15	The Campaign in France and Belgium	115
16	The Capture of Antwerp and on into Holland and Germany	123
17	Schleswig-Holstein and Luxembourg	139
	Honours and awards to officers and other ranks of the 13th HAC	149
	Postscript	151
	Brigadier Daniell, honours	152

ILLUSTRATIONS

Frontispiece	The author	
Plate 1	Pencraig	14
Plate 2	First steeplechase on Studley, Sandown 1921	23
Plate 3	The Manula man-eating Tiger	34
Plate 4	India 1924	42
Plate 5	Polo at Saugor	49
Plate 6	Equitation School, Saugor	51
Plate 7	Map of East Africa	56
Plate 8	The Grave of Frank Spurrell, Kibaya	61
Plate 9	Betty Daniell	85
Plate 10a	Map of Libya and Egypt	88
Plate 10b	Sketch map The Battle of Barrani	88
Plate 11	Map of Libya	92
Plate 12	Rommel	95
Plate 13	The author in the desert	98
Plate 14	Sketch map of 'Flank march of 500 miles'	103
Plate 15	German Tiger Tank	106
Plate 16	Map of Tunis	107
Plate 17	George IV reveiwing units of the 7th Armored Division	110
Plate 18a	Map of Caen, France	116
Plate 18b	Col. Bob's tank coming ashore in France	116
Plate 19a	The Bocage	118
Plate 19b	The Bocage	118
Plate 20	Map of the Netherlands	123
Plate 21	Brigadier Roscoe Harvey	124
Plate 22a	Sketch map of France and Belgium, 1944	126
Plate 22b	Antwerp	126
Plate 23	Map of Northern Germany	131
Plate 24a	British prisoners liberated by the author	135
Plate 24b	German prisoners	135
Plate 25	The author, Lindhof	141
Plate 26a	Lindhof	142
Plate 26b	The author's dachshund, Riki	142

Plate 27	Possibly the last picture of Hitler, 1945	144
Plate 28	Personal message from the C-in-C	147
Plate 29	Honorable Corps of Gentlemen at Arms	153
Plate 30	The author, Gentleman at Arms	154

Maps used as illustrations in this book were found amongst Brigadier Daniell's papers, now in the imperial War Museum; some appear to have been taken from unidentified newspapers of the day. Regrettably it has not been possible to establish whether any copyrights exists in respect of these.

FOREWORD

by Brigadier C. B. Harvey, DSO

I am delighted to have the opportunity of writing a foreword to the memoirs of Brigadier R. B. Daniell, DSO. I first met Bob Daniell in 1928 in our steeplechasing days but it was not until 1942 in the Desert War that we became closely associated. Then, with our backs to the Nile to the day we reached Lübeck on the Baltic, we were seldom separated.

From the Nile to the Baltic is a long, long way. During this period Bob and I covered many weary and some dangerous miles and fought many battles together.

During the last two years when we took part in the Second Front, Brigadier Daniell commanded the 13th Regiment Honorable Artillery Company, Royal Horse Artillery. They were under my command when I commanded the 29th Armoured Brigade 11th Armoured Division.

I could not have wished for anyone better. He was efficient, loyal and brave. He was also blessed with a sense of humour – a very important asset in war.

Roscoe Harvey
March 1984

Chapter 1

THE BOY – 1912-1920

In the summer of 1912, and a very wet summer it was, my mother inherited from her mother a small Welsh farmhouse called Pencraig with four hundred acres attached, in the very centre of Anglesey off the north-west coast of Wales. The house was very old, built of stone and at its centre the walls were six feet thick. My forebear who purchased it built on two large wings which rather detracted from the look of the little farmhouse and, if it were not for those two wings, it is quite possible I should be living there today.

It was in the middle of a dense wood and my forebear added to the wood, planting trees surrounding the house except on the eastern side from which there was a magnificent view of the whole of the Snowdonia range, from Great Ormes Head to the Rivals. Immediately in front of the house was the most immense beech tree which shaded the house more than we liked but it was such a magnificent tree we could not think of doing away with it.

My sister, Clare, and I loved this place and we had the happiest life that two children could possibly have there. She had been born on new year's day 1900 in the Banqueting House at Hampton Court Palace. Our parents had rented a houseboat but at Christmas in 1899 the rain was torrential and the boat started to sink. Friends in the palace insisted that mother should be brought into the Banqueting House although there was no water or light there. So here it was, at the far end of the sunken gardens on the southern side of Hampton Court Palace overlooking the Thames, that my sister was born. It did her no harm: she is very strong, very well and very vigorous today. [Since the author wrote this, Clare died in 1994, in her ninety-fifth year.]

The original Pencraig farmhouse was owned in 1456 by a family called Poole. There was a young man of twenty-three and his two sisters aged twenty-four and eighteen. The church in the village was being partly dismantled for repair as young Poole went down to the river, which passed the church, to collect some shingle to make cement. He saw, lying beside the doorway, the door, some cut stone and a stone for holy water. He put them into his farm cart and took them back to Pencraig where he installed them at the entrance to his garden. Later, the priest came, saying that the church was ready for the door to be placed in its proper site and asking for its return. Young Poole refused; he had put it into the wall of his garden and there it would stay. The priest went away but returned two months later, saying, 'Now, young Poole, if you do not return the door to the house of God, I will curse you and your family.' Poole laughed at him and again refused to return the door. Another two months passed before the priest again tried but received a further refusal. So the priest stood in front of the house, saying: 'I curse you by the bell and the book and within a month all three of you will be in the churchyard.' Within a month all three were dead and there is a plaque in the church to record their deaths within a few days of each other that year. Fortunately that curse did not extend to us and our family!

Pencraig

Our predecessor had planted several strips of trees on the estate and some copses but none really big enough to shelter game, which was a great sorrow to me.

My mother's family, the Phibbs, were from Southern Ireland. All her forebears were soldiers and most commanded or served in the Royal Irish Fusiliers, the old 87th. My father was English and he came from a family of East Indiamen. Sir James Daniell founded the trading post of Masulipatam (now called Machilipatnam), a couple of hundred miles north of Madras. They all had the ordinary furniture of the period which today would be priceless but at that time they thought nothing of it; all has disappeared.

The house and estate were originally purchased by Sir Richard Griffith, a man of great talent. He was the head of the Land Department in Dublin and he drew up himself the four famous maps of the land in Ireland and its value. Only two remain: one was found in an inn in Kerry by the authorities in Dublin, and we have the other. It now belongs to my brother who stoutly refuses to return it to Dublin. Sir Richard was an expert on land, knowing the value of every kind of land. He anticipated that the ways the Irish peasants grew their potatoes would lead to disease which would cause crop failures and terrible famine, with riots and much trouble. He therefore went to the nearest place across the sea, Anglesey, where he bought this farm which had excellent land, surrounded by a ring road.

The famine and riots came in Ireland and he sent his wife and children over to Pencraig. The extraordinary part of this great famine in Ireland was that, while thousands were dying with no food at all, every estate went on exporting corn to the United States which was desperately needed at home. Sir Richard instituted soup kitchens and he persuaded all the big landowners to enclose their estates with great walls so that stone-masons could at least earn a little money and save their families from utter destruction by starvation.

After the famine was over, he was a very tired man so he took his chief clerk in a brougham and they set off on a grand tour of Europe. He was not in the least interested in frivolous things, spurning Italy and southern France and travelled to what became Czechoslovakia. He was interested in land and one day in pouring rain they were going through mountainsides covered with pine trees when he told the coachman to stop. He asked his clerk to go to the nearest village and to buy a thousand hectares of this land, because, he said, 'If this land isn't carboniferous, then I know nothing about land.' Years later his son received a deputation from this part of the world asking if they could explore for minerals. He suddenly realised that this land which his father had bought and forgotten about must indeed be of value – the centre of it is where the Skoda works are today. Eventually, Sir Richard's son faced law suits as the Czechoslovaks did not want the best land in their country to belong to a foreigner. When he died, his widow was offered £100,000 – an absolute fortune in those days – to relinquish her interest in the land, which she did.

Sir Richard Griffith was a very great man. Little is known about him, but what he did, he did well. When he bought Pencraig and the small estate around it, he certainly did well.

In 1912 the island of Anglesey was years behind the rest of Great Britain. No telephones, no electric lights and not a single house had a bathroom. We all bathed in baths in our bedrooms and every night everyone who stayed in the house had his own silver candlestick to go to bed. Only one oil lamp at night didn't make any difference because we were all far too tired in the evening to dream of doing anything except wait for dinner and go to bed. The island had only a few families who lived in large stone-built houses and a lot of small farmers with very little acreage of very small fields.

The farmers could not have been nicer to my sister and me. We were, of course, foreigners because the language of Anglesey was Welsh. We seemed to be the only ones who spoke English and, although we had been there for three generations, we were still foreigners. I am not really sure that they were particularly kind to other foreigners.

The Royal Charter, which was a three-masted schooner on the way back from Australia carrying the first men home from the gold fields (every man wore a belt stuffed with gold dust), anchored off Moelfre Bay before going in to Liverpool. A storm rose and the ship was driven on to the land, the bowsprit being actually on dry land. Many farmers living nearby went down to see what was happening. It was recorded that there was not one survivor out of the eight hundred on board. Within a few days everyone on the island descended on Moelfre Bay and stripped that ship. Everyone had something. We had the captain's lantern which hangs outside my door here today. My uncle had a billiard table, the Pritchards had the captain's dining table and chairs, and every farmhouse had a porthole which was put into the bull pen. When the ship was recognised as a wreck, the Lutine Bell was rung in London and the assessors came to find absolutely nothing left except the bare boards and the rigging.

Moelfre Bay is ill-omened. Years later the submarine Thetis was beached there. I walked round it but I did not go inside as I knew there were twenty-one gallant men dead inside.

I was ten and Clare was twelve and we loved every stick and stone of Pencraig. Of course Sir Richard Griffith had added very much to the woodland round the house; the wood was extensive and most trees were very old. The gardens were walled and full of luscious pears, peaches and lovely flowers, but above all at the back of the house was a very large farmyard that Sir Richard had built of solid stone – huge barns, cow-houses, ladder-houses and everything you could think of. They were as good in my day as when he had built them. It was a wonderful place for us.

A thousand rooks lived in the trees around the house and he was a lucky man in the spring who got up the drive without being splattered!

At this time, our life was restricted by as far as we could walk but in my grandmother's day it was even more constrained. Solemn prayers at nine o'clock and every day in summer, not until three o'clock did we drive out in the wagonette, solid steel wheels and all, pulled by a charming pair of bays. Frequently we visited neighbours and had a wonderful meal in the kitchen. Six miles was the limit of these excursions.

The island had been denuded of trees by the Romans when it is said they flushed out and killed all the Druids. This left the island very windswept and very rocky but the land around Pencraig was very fertile and the spring lambs and black cattle from Ireland thrived on the grass. The north of the island was very rocky, with deep clear water and very cold. The south had sunny beaches and lovely sandy bays. Holyhead Island was just too far for us. Down the centre of the island ran the marsh and at one time I am quite sure it went right through to the other side of Red Wharf Bay. Thankfully it survived the efforts of German prisoners of war in 1915 who were brought over to dig dykes and drain it.

The women of Anglesey would not stand for these Germans and, the second day they were there, every woman advanced with her bread knife. The Germans fled and never came back, so the dykes were never built and the marsh was never drained. It is a haven for every form of wild fowl, herons, otters and, of course, hundreds of snipe. Bogs and marshes were to be found everywhere, each with its snipe and other wild life.

The only mark the Romans left was the grass of Parnassus, a charming flowering member of the saxifrage family whose seeds the Romans must have brought, involuntarily, from marshy ground elsewhere, in the saddles of their packhorses. Wherever they went on their roads on the island these flowers flourish and bloom every August.

There are only two battlefields known and marked; they have never been built over or made into grass of any sort and many people have looked for Roman remains on them but I don't think much was ever found.

I loved the spring best. Every day I went searching for plovers' eggs. I loved these, though they were hard to find but marvellous to eat, with that wonderful absolutely translucent whitish blue colour.

My favourite haunts were the small bogs that just had two or three plovers and a couple of snipe nesting. I would watch the nest: first one egg, then two, until they had their full crop of four. I would always leave at least one egg. Very soon I learnt not to be confused by the little nests that the cock made all round the nest of the female. It was indeed a day of jubilation for me when I found my first snipe's nest; all the little bogs had nests and with the snipe sitting on her eggs she was impossible to see.

The coast of Anglesey was full of sea birds. In the north there were Arctic and Roseate terns and in the south there was every known breed of seagull. Sea magpies nested in every bay. It was indeed a marvellous place for a small boy.

Clare and I rode out every day on our ponies and in the spring we used to go down to the very large Red Wharf Bay. The water went out a long way and we cantered along the sands, with the cuckoos calling from each side of the bay in the bright sunlight and the island covered with gorse. It was an idyllic spot.

In the summer, my serious job was shooting rabbits with a .22 rifle; I used to go to my friend Cyril Vivian and stalk rabbits on his land. There were thousands there and great fun it was.

We used to take picnics down to the sea, sometimes to bathe in the icy cold of the north but normally to the warm sandy beaches on the south. Then came the winter and that was the time when I never had a spare moment. I set off every day with my gun and searched around our own property first in every place I knew where there would be snipe and after that I wandered further afield, down to Hirdre-faig, the ugliest house I have ever seen, but it bordered on the marsh and so had great possibilities for me for duck and perhaps a pheasant. A few miles north of us was a very old house called Henblas and the couple who lived there were also very old. He had been wounded as an ensign in the Battle of Balaclava in the famous Charge of the Light Brigade. He was bearded and enormous. They had both grown old in this house and it was the quietest and most peaceful place I have ever known.

I used to go there on my bicycle to shoot. I went round their little woods wherever I thought there might be a rabbit or possibly a pheasant. One day, near the house, out of a bush sprang a bird which I didn't recognise. I shot it, picked it up and took it back. They told me it was a woodcock. My first woodcock, I couldn't have been more delighted.

So it continued every day. I sallied forth and went as far as I could and perhaps got a brace of snipe, possibly a rabbit or a duck and I couldn't have been more satisfied. Why I never had a dog I simply do not know. We never had shooting dogs but there were always dogs in the house though they were utterly useless to me and I never thought of asking my father for a shooting dog. It would have been a great help to me. I could hear the geese go over but could never find where they alighted. I knew they spent the night at Red Wharf Bay. I often went out in the early morning to get a shot at them as they came through but a .410 is not much use against a gaggle of geese!

And so our happy life at Pencraig went on year after year, interrupted by this terrible business of going to school which I disliked enormously. However, I survived because in the end I knew I would get back to Pencraig and all that it offered me.

Then the war came in 1914. The horses went as chargers for the army and a Canadian timber team arrived with their huge great horses and cut down two hundred trees. We were left, thankfully, with our new bicycles so we could at least get out a little further than we had been able to hitherto. An aerodrome was made and they brought in 'blimps' which were small airships; they were totally unsuited to the island and its sudden winds. The idea was that they were to go up, carrying a brave man who would watch for German submarines in the Irish Sea. Unfortunately the winds got up so quickly that they were unable to land and were blown far afield and the men drowned.

One day I saw one of those blimps in obvious trouble; the wind had risen and it was being driven out to sea. I cycled after it and saw it hit the ground on the shore of Red Wharf Bay. The pilot was out in a flash trying to deflate it and hold on to it at the same time. I hung on to another rope and we were both pulled far out across the sands before the whole thing collapsed. The excitement was terrific. We then had to lug it back to the foreshore and anchor it firmly to a small tree. Then I set off for home and tea.

Early in January 1916 there was a severe night frost, a very rare occurrence in Anglesey, and the marsh was frozen over. Next morning, a perfect, still, brilliantly sunny day, with frost in the air and on the ground, I set off in search of snipe. Every ditch and little bog were alive with them. Where I usually found a couple, twenty got up together. I lost my head and missed badly; then I got two with one shot and this miracle sobered me, so that I soon had enough snipe for the family, not that they really appreciated them. In the long grass tufts, the rabbits were lying out. I shot a couple and then my cartridges were finished.

This countryside held everything I loved most – the absolute stillness broken only by the trilling cry of the curlew, the piping of a red shank and, on this cold winter's morning, the mysterious and haunting cry of the pinkfooted geese travelling south low overhead, once heard never to be forgotten. From this day, the lure of the wild things, fur or feather, their ways and their cries, were written in my ten-year old heart and have remained with me all my life. In the heat of the Indian jungles I thrilled to the cough of a leopard and stood like a stone in Africa as the full-bodied roar of a hungry lion resounded around me, to be answered by the wicked scream of an old bull elephant with the limitless African bush stretching out to the distant horizon.

Years later in the days of the second world war, the ability to become an unrecognisable object was to stand me in good stead; when man was hunting man, it was the first one who shot who survived.

Always I have shot and hunted alone. Clare had a pony and she spent her happy days hunting. I only had the milkman's pony after his daily round, and galloping across the country was not encouraged.

My uncle, Colonel William Phibbs, DSO, died of wounds in France, commanding the old 87th, the Royal Irish Fusiliers. He was one of the best-looking men of his day as Field Marshal Lord Templer told me. He was buried with full military honours in the village churchyard.

Inevitably the years rolled by and our horizons lengthened and our friends increased. I went to St Aubyn's, which I really enjoyed, and on to Gresham's School in Holt, Norfolk, which I bore with fortitude. Finally I passed into the Royal Military Academy at Woolwich, where the discipline was unbelievable and the life very spartan indeed. But for me, at last I knew I was on my way to becoming a soldier.

Chapter 2

THE SOLDIER

I passed out of the Royal Military Academy seventh of my term, next to Charles Dalton, having attained the rank of cadet sergeant. Neither of us would accept the Royal Engineers. So it was that shortly after Christmas, I was posted and joined in 1921 the 1st Battery Royal Artillery, known as 'The Blazers'. I was met at Aldershot station by Driver Fortune in the battery dog-cart. There were four batteries making up the regiment; the officers were just back from Ireland as the 'Black and Tans' and were most welcoming. I loved every moment of my life, even riding at the head of the daily exercise in pouring rain and sleet.

One morning I was instructed to take the trap and Driver Fortune and go over to the RAF mess at Farnborough, there to pick up the hub-caps of the gun wheels which they had buffed for us.

The mess-room was full of bored RAF pilots and my arrival seemed to them like a gift from heaven. I was ushered in and placed on a window seat. When asked if I would like a drink, I said a small beer. At least twenty officers got up and set off to get my small beer. It seemed very good and, when invited to have another, I accepted. Little did I know what they had concocted. A reverential hush descended on everyone as I started to taste my second brew. Something very unusual shook me and I disappeared out of the window amid tumultuous applause. Then came the mounting of the dog-cart: as I climbed up one side, I pushed Driver Fortune out of the other. This went on for some time until I was finally picked up amid wild cheers and bundled in somehow.

For some days I was very ill and wished only for an early death. I recovered but have never since been able to drink a pint of beer. This has been a great trial to me.

To my great delight, I acquired a charming little brown mare as my charger and now I could join the other officers hunting two days a week with the South Berks and on Fridays, when possible, with that gallant old Colonel Shackle's very swift staghounds.

I shared a very small room with Bill Morgan, who became my life-long friend, though he always had some disparaging remark to make as I brought out photographs of my latest girl – such as, 'She's got a squint!'

I learnt no gunnery at all. Where the shells went once they left the gun I had no idea but fortunately Salisbury Plain is very large. I could have won the Lightweight Race at the army point-to-point, if my excitement could be controlled. Actually I fell on my head!

Gerry Shiell was Mrs Marr's favourite nephew. She owned a famous stud in Co. Kildare and at this time Gerry had two good steeplechasers, but things had not gone right for him. He had several crashing bad falls, finally breaking a collar bone and two ribs. He asked me to try and keep his horses fit and at the same time suggested I should purchase a sound jumper to run at Sandown in the Royal Artillery Gold Cup in April. He found Studley for me. On the great day Clare came down to Sandown and I had a glorious and safe ride, finishing last, for I had no idea how much hard work my gallant horse needed.

From that momentous day, one of my aims in life was born – to win the Gunner Gold Cup. I achieved this twice but it took me a long time and I was taught how hard it is to win a steeplechase if you are an impecunious subaltern.

The colonel sent for me one morning and said, 'Bob Daniell, have you ever been to a hunt ball?'

'No, sir,' said I.

'Well,' he said, 'You will go to the Warwickshire Hunt Ball on Friday. I will lend you my pink evening coat. You will escort my god-daughter. She is married. Here is their address and £3 for your rail ticket. Write and say when you will arrive.'

Everything went to plan. I got there and was met by Eileen's charming father, who never changed gear in his car which he drove flat out, shooting off into a field if he couldn't make a corner. I liked his very attractive daughter, much enjoyed the ball and, in spite of a dreadful hang-over, fell madly in love with her.

Her father was an old Brazilian estate owner. He bought Deddington Manor, with the famous Kineton Brook running through it. He immediately divided his four hundred acres into four fields of a hundred acres each, and every morning we both set out on ponies to count the stock. I spent several weekends there and got to know the family well. Eileen's father and I spent many hours digging an artificial 'earth' in his covert, and it was occupied later that spring to his immense satisfaction. We also improved the banks of the Kineton Brook, making it a safer but probably bigger jump for the brave. He showed me how to break a totally wild pony in a day and taught me to use the Brazilian three-balled rope for lassoing wild steers: all the greatest fun.

Then Eileen asked me to go to Switzerland for ten days with her. That really stirred up trouble. Mother came up to London to see us off and take stock of this woman and she certainly was not eased when she found that I had given Eileen my sleeper. She need not have worried, for we were good friends and remained just that. Maybe this was due to the presence in our pension of a charming and most attractive Viennese countess of eighteen years. She was an expert skier, which I was not, but I could just manage to keep up with her. Eileen was just hopeless. Bobs Acland, the scientist, came to stay for a few days. One morning at day break, we climbed slowly out of the valley on skis. Our object was to reach the refuge hut on the Pleine Morte Glacier and there to stay the night. To say that this expedition was lunatic on the part of Bobs and myself is to put it mildly. The guide must have been mad, for it was a formidable climb and the snow was bad. I suppose someone looks after idiots for, as the sun was sinking and all the peaks around us were pink, we rushed the glacier and then, led by the countess who flew past me like a swallow, we reached the hut as darkness fell.

It was far too cold to sleep. When daylight came, we could not see a yard so we had to stay put. However, after a horrifying trip across the glacier, roped to each other, we eventually had a rift in the clouds and far, far below us we saw the village from which we had set out. I felt sick when I saw the edge of the precipice on which we stood and vowed, if we did make the village, I would never, never ski up into the mountain tops again, however attractive my companions. I never have.

During my races on Studley, I met several officers of the Royal Horse Artillery Regiment. I was much impressed by their charm, prowess and obvious ability. I then decided that my second aim in life was to get my 'jacket' and be posted to the Royal Horse Artillery. The RHA was formed in 1793 and the officers and men were selected from the Royal Regiment of Artillery as a whole, earning their place within the RHA by their conduct and professionalism. The first RHA jackets were of a French open style with flat buttons, but by 1804 RHA officers and soldiers wore ball buttons (as they do to this day – unlike their RA counterparts) in three rows. On joining an RHA regiment officers have historically referred to 'winning' or 'earning' their jacket. I never veered from this for a day and some years later, on my return from India, I was duly posted to 'D' Battery, Royal Horse Artillery.

A couple of days after returning from Switzerland, I was packed off with my groom, my batman and my two horses to a small artillery range near Dundee. No one else wanted to go but they were wrong for it was a wonderful wild place. It ran alongside a firth, good firm sand, ideal for galloping, the sea full of inquisitive grey seals. It was a lovely spring, with the eider duck nesting all over the sand dunes. I was not hard worked and busied myself building a mile gallop with four good fences. I tried to catch trout in the burns, to no avail.

My job was ideal. My groom and I cantered some three miles along the shore to a lighthouse where I sat at the top window reporting by telephone, if I was looking, where shells burst with reference to the target. I had much to distract me – fat eider duck wandering along to their nests, counting the grey seals and eating a fabulous Scottish lunch brought up to me by the wife of the lighthouse keeper – so I just reported rather too many dud shells.

*First Steeplechase on Studley
Sandown 1921*

Then, one Sunday, when everyone else had gone away, I had an invitation to tea at the Guthrie's who lived nearby at Carnoustie. They were a charming family and Jean, their eldest daughter and I soon became bosom friends. Every day when there was no shooting, Jean cycled over and we set off for a gallop over the fences, along the sands and into the countryside. I became devoted to Jean but, alas, our paths soon parted. We went to the county horse show, where Jean, to her immense joy, won the jumping competition on my brown mare with a prize of £5.

Back to Aldershot with no time to think and next day the regiment marched off to Salisbury Plain at day-break, bivouacking a night on the way.

Practice camp can be a severe test for a gunner regiment but to me at this stage it was the greatest fun. The night before I was to have my first shoot, Bill Morgan lectured me for a long time after I was asleep in his maddening Irish brogue on what I was supposed to do. Thankfully all went satisfactorily – the shells exploded near the wooden bridge target and not among the generals, which can indeed happen.

My father very surprisingly gave me a single cylinder Triumph motor cycle which, now the summer was approaching, made all the difference to my enjoyment of life.

I went to the summer ball at Sandhurst and there had the good fortune to pair up with Crystal Hawkshore. Her parents had the most lovely house at Liphook, at the top of the hill, overlooking the countryside right down to the sea. I was there constantly for tennis, dances or just to be with Crystal. Her large circle of most attractive girls kept me enthralled all the summer. Very wisely her mother forbade me to take any of them on the back of my Triumph, so we could not stray far.

I hadn't seen Gerry Shiell for some months. I knew he was hoping to marry a Miss Macdonald who was a very charming and good looking girl but he had to wait for his mother to come over from Ireland to see that she could ride well enough to be a member of the Shiell family. This she duly did and Gerry married her. Then our ways parted and I am sorry to say I didn't see him again for several years, for I admired him enormously. It was in the desert one evening before the Battle of Akarit that I saw Gerry walking straight towards the German lines. The only thing I could do was to fire a couple of smoke-shells and drop them as close to him as I could. I did this and fortunately he had the sense to realise that someone was trying to help; he turned round and walked back. We had a chat together for a short time and then again the years passed before we met next. The day before we crossed the Rhine in 1945, I heard that he was close by, so I went to see him, had dinner with him and we had a very pleasant evening. Neither of us had any idea that he would be dead next morning, blown up on a mine. There were not many mines in that area; it was really a tragedy and I was very sorry when I heard about it.

One day after lunch at Aldershot, the colonel collected all the officers in the mess to tell us that the War Office had requested a volunteer to go to India. No one volunteered. He then turned to me and said, 'Bob, what about you?'

'Well,' I said, 'Colonel, this regiment has been everything to me, everybody has been charming to me and I am very happy here so I would hate to leave the regiment. Can you tell me if the regiment is likely to come to India in the next few years?'

The colonel replied, 'Well, I did ask the War Office that and they said we wouldn't be sent to India for another six years.'

'Well,' I said, 'I know I am destined to go to India and I will volunteer, for I come from a family of East Indiamen and I know that I must go to India.' My forebear, Probyn, was a great figure in the Mutiny; he raised an irregular cavalry regiment and achieved tremendous renown. The colonel said I would get some embarkation leave and would probably sail about the 1st March.

I duly had a fortnight's leave and I went back to Pencraig. Everything was exactly as I had left it, such a long time ago. I got my kit together but could not find my great coat. I asked my father if he had seen it. He said, 'Of course I haven't seen it. I paid a great deal of money for it. Have you pawned it?'

'Oh,' I said, 'Yes, I did. With Moss Bros.'

'What did they give you for it?'

'Thirty shillings,' I replied.

'Well, I paid £29 for it and this I will not have!' Some days later he was to be seen top hatted and striding towards Moss Bros to get the coat back. His arrival must have caused a stir as they gave him the coat and refunded the £3 necessary to redeem it.

In early March of 1922 the whole family came down to see me off on a dreadful little trooper called the Worcestershire in which we suffered most awful seas in the Bay of Biscay. The boat was full of soldiers and every single one was sick. Until we reached the lovely weather of the Mediterranean that ship was a misery. I went ashore at Port Said and bought the usual rubbish. I was accosted by a smelly man who produced a pack of cards and said, 'These cards are marked with fifty-two ways of making love.' Now, I was extremely ignorant and I thought this would be very useful to me. I gave him ten shillings and when I opened them carefully in my cabin every single one was blank!

We journeyed on and each day became finer and warmer, the nights darker, the stars brighter and I was happier. I knew I had been foolish to volunteer. I had been told that to volunteer for anything in the army was usually suicide but indeed I was foolish because my regiment, where I had been so happy, happened to come out to India some three months after me and they went to the three best stations in India, namely Meerut, Bareilly and Mathura.

To my great disappointment, no mermaids were to be seen as we passed Aden. The ship still smelled abominably and I think every man on board was longing to reach Bombay. At length one pearly morning, the ship stopped and we were there. Ashore in the roseate dawn, I saw the huge archway of the Gateway to India and there was India beyond it.

Chapter 3

INDIA

Disembarkation was complete chaos. Just as I was about to descend the gangway, a small Indian in spotless white approached me and said, 'Sahib, I am your bearer. I will look after you. I'll serve you and I will collect your luggage while you go to Army and Navy Stores and order camp kit. All most essential. The train leaves at 4 p.m. for Kirkee and Poona.'

I was too hot to worry, so I signed for various unbelievable articles of equipment and duly reached Bombay station. The first thing that surprised me was that, although there were countless hordes of Indians milling about, no one at all was in a hurry. My bearer, name unknown, arrived, luggage arrived and, to crown it all, the enormous number of camp kit items arrived too.

The scenery was marvellous as we crawled up the Western Ghats; lush greenery and huge trees such as I was never to see again. Suddenly, no more vegetation, just a sandy plain and rocky hills. The train just stopped and I got out. I had arrived. No visible station and no one to meet me. It turned out to be Kirkee, my destination.

My bearer quickly commandeered a bullock cart for my two trunks and suggested that I rode in it. 'Certainly not,' I said and strode off, followed by a long line of next-to-naked children carrying my camp kit. The last one, three years old, carried my lantern, which to his great delight was lit and this entailed sitting down every few yards to marvel at his good fortune.

The whole place was pitch dark. A light appeared in the darkness and I soon reached the welcome of the doctor and his wife. I was not impressed with my new quarters, although the whisky was good and I liked my hostess.

Next day I discovered I was in a very pleasant quiet place, lots of small bungalows each set in its own compound with garden, stables and go-downs. The lines and battery stables were about a mile away. It was a lovely day and not too hot. The whole place was a mass of the lovely flame of the forest trees in full bloom. I gathered that the regiment stationed here had left for England a week before and my new regiment was due to arrive from Quetta in a month or so. To my care were left several hundred horses, a few mules and a number of Indian drivers, Punjabi-Mussulmans, fortunately with their own Indian officers and NCOs. A cheerful lot, but of course I could not understand one word they said.

I spent a pleasant morning every day in the horse lines. I counted the horses but the total was never the same two days running. The mules I treated with great respect as they kicked and bit for no reason at all. The Indian officer always accompanied me, wearing a magnificent turban and he was very helpful to me. He allotted me an excellent polo pony on which I learned to play the game. He produced a young orderly who was even keener on shooting than myself. After lunch I slept for an hour and then rode off on my pony to explore the place. I found a charming club on the banks of a fair-sized river, which I joined. I rode into the large native city at Poona one evening where, knowing nothing, I saw nothing of its native treasures, not even the Mahratta Chieftain, the Pleshwa's Palace. I thought it very noisy, very dirty and very smelly. This was a pity because it put me off exploring the colourful cities up and down the sub-continent of India.

On my way home in front of me was a small and somewhat dilapidated two-horse trap. The driver sat in front and the occupants, an Indian man and woman behind. After a couple of miles, the woman drew aside her sari, opened her legs and gave birth to a child. The husband jumped down, ran along behind, collected the child and jumped in again. The driver never even turned round nor did the pony stop trotting. I certainly was astonished but I had seen so many astonishing sights since I landed, it didn't really mean much to me.

The new regiment duly arrived. They were extremely efficient: the detrainment went without a hitch, the men were fed and installed in their huge barracks, all the officers in their various bungalows – before dinner. I did not really take to any of my brother officers. They were uninterested in shooting, playing polo or pig-sticking and, after a year or two in Iraq, only asked for a quiet life. A few days later, the adjutant sent for me. He was a man I cordially disliked and I am quite sure the dislike was mutual. He told me that the colonel had agreed that I should take over the mess and I was to check the silver, the glass, china and all the paraphernalia that was contained in the mess buildings. I was specially to check the kitchens and the cooking arrangements, going through the mess bills and the accounts. I think the adjutant thought I would dislike this very much; actually it suited me very well. It fitted in with my early morning shooting plans as I didn't have to get back till quite late in the morning. My first week went quite pleasurably: I checked the silver which was in an enormous book and had last been checked by an elderly officer in 1856, the year before the Indian Mutiny. He had done it thoroughly but he wasn't to live long: he was butchered and his body was laid on the mess table.

The mess consisted of the mess room, like every other mess room, furnished with comfortable leather furniture, only used in the rains, and a very nice fern-strewn arbour where we had a glass of Madeira before meals. The mess itself was a large room with open sides on to a verandah, a huge punkah pulled by a little boy with a piece of rope through a hole in the wall. He lay on his back and pulled it with his toes; he frequently went to sleep and was jerked very unpleasantly to make him work a bit harder. There were no heads because there wasn't room for them. Surrounding it there were trees and what might have been a garden. There was a large compound with many go-downs inhabited by at least two hundred people and, as there were only eight mess servants, all the people who lived there must have been distant relations of the men who looked after us in the mess.

Finally, in the second week I got down to the accounts. These were kept by a very old man on a high stool in a dark little room, the windows of which had never been opened. The first thing he asked me to do was to sign a cheque for forty gallons of oil; I said, 'What on earth are forty gallons of oil for?' He said they were used in the lamp in the mess. I said, 'There is only one small lamp that couldn't use four gallons, let alone forty!'

Of course, at the time, I never thought that all the people in the go-downs used the mess oil for their lamps. I told him I would not sign for more than four gallons to which he responded, 'Oh, very good, sahib. If you say so, that shall be so.'

I then tried to find the kitchens, but there did not seem to be any! Over perhaps a hundred or a hundred and fifty years, the cooks seemed to cook wherever they happened to be. I asked to see the cook, but he was away buying food and I never found him, nor did I ever find where he cooked but, whoever did cook, cooked on small charcoal fires. I had never done any cooking on charcoal fires so I really couldn't do much about it. I altered the menus, I got rid of the rice and curry which I didn't like and all went well.

On the first day of the next week, we were just about to stand up to drink the loyal toast, which was a very solemn moment in the mess. All the candles had been extinguished leaving just the oil lamp giving out a very small light, when that light suddenly died. The colonel was furious, sent for the kitmahgar who said, 'Oh, sahib, the new mess secretary, sahib, say no oil, so lamp goes out.' Naturally the colonel was very angry and said that he didn't want his daily life in any way disturbed and, if the lamp needed forty gallons of oil a month, it needed forty gallons and that is what it would have.

I was most interested in the silver. It had been extremely well detailed and I discovered it all belonged to the John Company of the Bombay Troop of Horse Artillery and the John Company of the Madras Horse Artillery. It was all Queen Anne silver, brought to India in the time of Clive. I was very ignorant about silver. I thought it must be valuable but I had no idea of its enormous value. I was interested to see that not a single knife or fork or any single piece of silver had been lost or stolen. There were quite a lot of silver cups of various kinds; one was the Kadir Cup: I looked at it and thought that, next to the National, I'd love to win that Kadir Cup. I found that the table had been sold during the last war to an astute Indian who paid very little for it and sold it back to the mess after the war for ten times what he had paid. It was a lovely table with twelve leaves and on eight of these leaves were the outlines of the eight officers who had been butchered in the Mutiny and had been laid out on the table. I have often tried to see shadowing of the wood. I imagined I did but it wasn't very easy to see.

Round the mess room was a colonnade and that could be shut by sliding glass windows. Now they were only used in the rains to keep out the flying ants and other horrors – also to exclude the cobras of which there was a vast number always around the mess room. Sitting in the arbour on the Sunday morning, I happened to look up and saw the most enormous and horrible-looking cat on one of the rafters, looking down at me. He was surrounded by at least twenty lesser cats. I discovered that there were cats all over the place so on the Monday I said to the steward that all these cats must go. 'They are to be collected up, put in a sack and I personally shall take them away to the bazaar and sell them to people who want to have a cat.'

'Very good, sahib, as you say, it shall be done.'

Two or three nights later, just as we had passed the solemn moment of drinking the health of the king and sat down again, there was the most frightful noise: tom-toms beating, flares going all over the place and myriads of small boys dashing about. The colonel asked the kitmahgar what was happening and he replied, 'Oh, everybody catch cats, because the new mess president, he said all cats must go, so everybody catch cats.' The mess was invaded by fleeing cats, followed by little boys and the noise was indescribable. The colonel got up and left, tripping over a little boy who had just caught a cat, and stalked out. Next day, he told the adjutant that he was too old for this and that I must be told to lessen my enthusiasm with regard to the mess. However I did collect the cats in three or four sacks. I sent them to the bazaar which was eight miles away and I hoped never to see them again.

In the mess was a pleasant vet called Colonel Argyll and one morning he said, 'Bob, would you like to come with me at five o'clock this evening if I pick you up in my trap. He took me to the churchyard and showed me various graves and said, 'Bob, read those gravestones and you will find they are all ensigns, all young men between nineteen and twenty. They were all dead in a few months after they came out here and they all had cats on their minds. Now, if I were you, I'd forget about cats.' Well, I tried, but when I was sitting in the arbour on the next Sunday, sure enough that dreadful old cat was there and all the other cats had come back too. However, I respected Colonel Argyll enormously so I did what he told me and I couldn't care less. You see the cats did keep down the rats and they did frighten away the snakes.

My last effort to modernise the mess and the mess compound was to order that everyone who was not connected with the eight men who served us in the mess must leave. They responded magnificently. Just as we were getting up from the mess, they produced professional wailers from the bazaar at Poona, bullock carts, tom-toms and all. The adjutant then told me that the colonel had heard from a cousin of mine who was a great friend of his, Colonel Fletcher Cruikshank, who was district commissioner for Gawal State in the Himalayas that if, at the time of this, my first hot weather, I was a bane and trouble to him, he could send me up there. He therefore agreed that on Friday evening I should leave.

I am quite sure my cousin Fletcher, of whom I was extremely fond, had no conception that this suggestion would ever be accepted. However, here I was on Bombay Station, on my way to Gawal. I had no idea where it was, I had no map, I didn't have to take a ticket as I had a warrant. I was shown into a very good compartment on the Punjab Mail. There was a certain amount of noise and confusion in the station, as it seemed to me there was a great number of people with red turbans and red waist-bands, bowing and scraping and so on. Why all this was going on, I didn't know.

Eventually, we set off and what made it so pleasant was that we stopped at stations to have our meals, breakfast, lunch and evening meal. The countryside enthralled me to start with but as the days and nights went past, I got more and more bored with it as it was just one enormous plain.

At every station where we stopped, the first thing to be done was to jump out of your compartment and lock your door, before the monkeys got in. At the first station, I didn't know anything about the monkeys and they pinched my shoes and I never did get them back.

One morning we stopped earlier than usual and the whole place was a mass of Indians, chanting, covered with garlands, conch shells blowing, tom-toms banging. The noise was fantastic and, as I opened my door to see what on earth was going on, to my amazement, there were three huge elephants just in front of the door. The middle one was kneeling down and had a painted howdah on it and a step ladder for someone to get up. About two hours later, the maharajah, who had travelled up in his private coach at the back of the Punjab Mail, came down covered with garlands. The noise was amazing as he walked slowly up to the elephant, mounted the steps and got into his howdah. After about another hour, the procession started off and away they went to the native city which must have been nearby. I think this was in Rajputana. Nothing of interest happened again for three or four days and nights but eventually we arrived at Peshawar where the station master took charge of me. My bearer had told me before I left that I was going too far away for him and his family; he feared to go so far away in case he never came home and he didn't really think that I would ever come home either.

The station master took me to a little train, much smaller than the Punjab Mail, and again we set off and travelled for another day and a night. It then stopped and I saw that we had arrived in the hills.

I got out and found a Gurkha subhadar with several other gurkhas; they looked like little boys with their ponies. He brought me a letter from Fletcher to say that he was going to look after me on my ride up from Kathagodarm railhead to

Almora, his station. We set off presently with baggage ponies and we rode up through the forest. It was marvellous to get into the shade and to the smell of the pine trees with a breeze sighing through the branches that I hadn't heard since I'd been to Scotland. It was hot but nothing like it was on the plains. We carried on like this for three days, spending the nights in dak bungalows which were very comfortable and we were served with very edible meals. The third night, the dak caretaker produced for me a dish of strawberries – little ones like those that used to be served in Switzerland; they look marvellous and I ate the lot! Next morning I was very ill because I ought to have washed them in potassium permanganate but I had no idea one had to do that. I had to stay there for two days as I was unable to move. On the second day the dak bungalow bearer brought me a milk pudding, beautifully made, that settled my stomach and cured me. I asked him where it came from and he said that it had been sent by the rajah's lady who lived about three hours ride away.

So the next day, instead of going on up the hill, we went off to find this rajah's lady to thank her for her very welcome rice. After about three and a half hours, we came to a clearing and a charming little cottage, thatched exactly like any village cottage in England, a semi-circle of lawn in front and three pine trees to the left. The cottage itself was covered with roses and there were lots of flowers all round. Out of the cottage came a charming elderly lady. She asked after my health and was very pleased to see me, inviting me to rest before having the lunch she had prepared for me.

As a girl of fifteen her father and mother had died of cholera down in the plains and the rajah had taken her into his household to look after his numerous children. She must have been very pretty by the poor photograph she showed me and I am quite sure the rajah fell deeply in love with her. Anyway she stayed there for thirty-five years by which time the children were grown up. The rajah asked if she would like to return to England but she replied, 'No, your highness, I would never want to go back to England now. I would like a little house up in the foothills of the Himalayas, so that I can look down on the plains of India and up to the mountains under their permanent snow.' He built the house and she moved to this marvellous spot, with absolute quiet while every month two bullock carts set out from the rajah's palace bringing food and all the things he thought she might need.

After an excellent lunch of pheasant, she asked if I would like to rest in the hammock which was stretched between two of the three pines. I got into the hammock and found it very comfortable until I looked down and there were the plains of India 8,000 feet below me. I immediately got out of the hammock and crawled back to the house on all fours because I had no head for heights. She wasn't sad or lonely; she had squirrels and birds that were very tame and she was happy. She was known as the rajah's lady and was highly respected throughout the district, No one would ever think of invading her privacy or doing anything other than helping her if she needed any assistance. I rode back and we set off again, finally reaching Almora a couple of days later.

I was delighted to see my cousin again. I wasn't so delighted to see his wife to whom I hadn't taken when they married and now they had a baby that never seemed to stop yelling. The bungalow was not large and with a baby screaming all the time I found it very trying. I tried to advise her that the reason for the screaming was that it did not have a balanced meal. What it did not eat for breakfast it had to eat for lunch and if that wasn't finished up then it was served again for dinner. You can't imagine what a mess the result was.

I got very bored there with no young people around. There was a large Gurkha barracks but no officers' wives with whom to play tennis. Fletcher realised this quickly and suggested I might like to go shooting. I jumped at the suggestion as I had brought my gun and plenty of ammunition. He gave me a subhadar whom he ordered to look after me.

We set off and rode for about two days to the more wooded part of the foothills. Here a series of hills ran parallel to each other, several thousand feet high and each a little higher than the one before. We were always walking up hill and down which was very tiring. We arrived at a bungalow which was comfortable with the forest all round us. Fletcher had told me that there were serowe, which were very rare indeed, and there were other small antelopes and pheasants and jungle cock, so he didn't think we would starve. Actually we got very hungry. The forest was fairly thick, mostly rhododendrons, with big fir trees. One evening some of the men came in and told us that a woman had been attacked and killed by a tiger. They thought that the tiger was the well-known man-eater that had been troubling that area for the last three years. They asked me if I would go to the village and try to shoot it. When we reached the village, the body had been taken away for burial and a young bullock had been put out as bait. The wise old tiger didn't come anywhere near us and we went home rather dejected.

I knew absolutely nothing about tigers. I knew nothing about dangerous game and I knew nothing about man-eaters. It was a pity because I was just about to learn it all.

Two mornings later we were out in the forest looking for antelope. There was a very dense thicket at the bottom of a valley and as we passed we heard a tiger growling, grunting and giving off small roars. I clambered as high as I could up the valley and got behind a tree with my subhadar. We waited to see what would happen. Nothing happened, so we went on looking for our antelopes. Undoubtedly it was the same tiger and undoubtedly it was a man-eater. Now tigers are only man-eaters because they have been badly wounded in some way. They may have porcupine spines through their paws or their mouths and they cannot catch the wild animals that they normally feed on so they turn to the lesser animal, the human who is very easy to kill in the forest when seeking kindling, or fruit to eat. Such tigers become extremely wise and they are very dangerous and difficult to shoot.

The Manula Man-eating Tiger

Two days later, three men came from different directions to say that a woman on her way home to the village in broad daylight had been killed by the tiger. She was lying below the path and they would leave her there if I would come and try to shoot the tiger. After having something to eat, I set out. It was about six miles away and when I arrived the local men showed me where the body was. They said they would build me a hide on the side of the path, among the rhododendron bushes which were very thick, about eight feet high. Below the rhododendrons the ground was completely open and there lay the tattered and half eaten body of the young girl, her torn sari fluttering in the breeze.

I didn't like it as, once seated, I literally couldn't move an inch. However, in my total ignorance, I visualised the tiger walking across the open ground on to his kill. Anyway, it was getting late and there were no trees nearby. The men from the village walked away and I was left alone. It was utterly silent as the evening drew on. The tiger, who was lying in the grass quite near, had witnessed all these goings-on many times before and he was extremely hungry. He walked noiselessly, unseen by me, down the centre of the path. When he got to the hide, he sat down a few feet below it. The first thing I knew was that the hairs on my neck stood up on end, a hot foetid air came up through my legs and loud stomach rumblings could be heard. I sat motionless; the tiger was undecided what to do, as though he could smell me but not see me. He climbed up the bank to have a closer look. Out of the corner of my eye, I could see his huge and wicked looking striped head about six feet behind me. I realised that he would get me long before I could get my rifle out of the branches, so I stayed where I was. He presently walked off down the path. I hoped he would come across the open fields below on to his kill but he didn't and I never saw him again.

As darkness fell, I shouted and kept on shouting until I heard the village men approaching with lanterns, making a lot of noise. They followed the pug marks of the tiger, with more and more amazement, and they attributed my amazing escape to believing that I must be very closely related to one of their forest gods who had been asleep for a long period and had woken up in the nick of time to save his off-spring.

What interested me more was that they said the man-eater would now go away and not return to their forest for several months. I am afraid I took this with some scepticism, so I invited four families to come and camp on the verandah of my forest bungalow, where I would pay them and promised them as much meat as they could eat. In return they were to keep a large fire burning all night. In the end the promise of meat was too tempting and the whole small village came.

I fancied they were correct in what they said. The tiger probably went a hundred miles away in the Terai below the foothills and was not seen again for many months. They thought he disliked being hunted; well, I sympathised with him, for neither did I.

I read of his death some three years later. He had been hunted without success by several very experienced forest officers, until one day in broad daylight, he was just beginning to eat a small boy in the middle of a village street, when a district officer rode by. The officer was rushed into a hut and had a simple point blank shot through a window. The tiger had a porcupine quill which had pierced both upper and lower jaws sometime before. His known number of human kills was recorded at twenty-two; poor chap he might so easily have made me his twenty-third!

I was severely shaken by this episode and, the more I thought about it, the less I liked it so I sent Fletcher a note by an Indian runner to say I was returning. That day I stayed indoors until the evening when I ventured out and had the good luck to shoot three small fat deer called gurral for the villagers. My mother had one of their skins as a mat by her bed until she died.

I recovered and set about looking for the mythical and rare serowe but I was not really interested, a pity as sure enough I stumbled on two of them. They were frozen in their tracks; so was I and in a trice they had vanished.

Fletcher then arrived with a company of Gurkhas, baggage ponies, food and tents. He said he was on his way up the Pindari Pass to a large village in Tibet, where a huge fair was held once every five years. He suggested that I should come too and had thoughtfully brought me thick underclothes and several Gurkha jerseys. It was a very pleasant march, along the well worn forest paths for three or four days though I had no chance to shoot anything. Fletcher shot a lot of pheasants on the ground. He never mentioned my escape from the Manaula man-eater and most probably did not believe a word of it. We averaged twenty to twenty-five miles a day.

Then one morning we arrived at a ravine, deep and rocky; it was crossed by a rope bridge, the like of which I had never seen before. One large strand of rope to walk on and side ropes to hold on to. To the Gurkhas it was as simple as crossing the Thames on Westminster Bridge; they just flowed across, each man carrying a huge pack. To me, when I watched the bridge swaying to and fro, my blood ran cold; however it had to be crossed so, taking off my boots, I set off with my face buried in Fletcher's back and conveniently passed out with sheer fright. We left one platoon of Gurkhas there, the pack ponies and all the baggage we could not carry. The Pindari Pass was quite close; as a pass it did not exist, just a goat track up a sheer rock face. I have no doubt it could have been worse, anyway it was a lovely day. Several tarrh were jumping about on the ledges. When we arrived at the top, I got a wildly excited Gurkha to sit on my legs while I leant over the precipice and had a shot at one of the goats or tarrh below. As I shot, it leapt into the air and crashed down; the Gurkha, yelling with excitement, jumped off my legs to see where it had landed and I, as near as an ace, followed it. Honour was satisfied, no more tarrh for me. It took two days to retrieve but it was excellent eating.

The Tibetan village was indescribable: several quite substantial but crazily built wooden houses, with hundreds of dreadful looking long-haired Tibetan men and no doubt an equal number of Tibetan women milling around. The smell of rancid ghee or butter, dirt and yak-dung fires was revolting. We camped about a mile away up-wind and immediately a dreadful looking ruffian appeared who would not leave Fletcher and me. It eventually transpired that he was a hunter and he wished to take me up into the snows to hunt snow leopard. He produced his yak and said I could ride it. I have never seen such a dreadful looking beast, a species of cow, with short legs, horns and matted hair hanging down to the ground. I declined the invitation. I didn't like the look of that man or the smell of his dreadful yak. I am sure all he wanted was to cut my throat and steal my rifle. He was obviously disappointed and suddenly produced a magnificent recently half cured skin of a lovely snow leopard. I fell for it and bought it from him. No sooner had I reached the plains than all the hair just fell off it.

My poor cousin Fletcher had to stay in this ghastly village for two weeks, just to show the flag. I left the following day with a platoon of Gurkhas but I absolutely refused to cross over the bridge. We just slid down the ravine and clambered up the other side. It took us two days but my goodness it was worth it. At the camp we met a fresh platoon going up with some supplies and very thankfully we set off for the depot at Almora. It was a very pleasant march and I much enjoyed it. The rhododendrons were coming out, the path was excellent, plenty of gurral about, and always in front of me were the snow-capped mighty Himalayan peaks.

We arrived back at Almora; Fletcher's wife seemed pleased to see me, her child still yelling its head off. Then I found a note from Fletcher's second in command asking me to come down to the railhead at Kathgodarm in the fast trotting mule mail cart. He hoped that I would arrive in time to catch the weekly train to Peshawar and take care of his wife who was returning to England for six months. We met up alright and I had an evening meal with them at the forest bungalow. I liked them both, especially his wife, who was young, dark and most attractive.

She and I set off in the little train for Peshawar next morning and transferred to the Bombay Mail. It wasn't much more than three weeks since I had arrived. I missed the coolness of the hills, the scent of the pine trees and all the happy little Gurkhas running about. By now it was the hot weather in earnest, about 110 degrees in the shade, if you could find it. We shared a first class compartment, a bunk on each side, a punkah, small closet and wash-basin. My companion then told me that she felt very ill and thought she was going to have a bad attack of dysentery. This indeed happened and here was I, madly shy, with a charming but very ill woman on my hands. I had never even seen a woman with no clothes on, in my life. I bathed her, I am sure very ineptly, to try to keep her temperature down, as often as she asked me and did my best to tend her. After several blistering days and nights, the Bombay Mail stopped one evening at the tiny station of Muttrah. The Sikh engine driver said that the train would stay there until six o'clock next morning; he did not say why.

The station master produced a carriage and helped me get my semi-conscious companion into it. We drove to the military hospital where the nurses took charge and I kissed her good-bye. I went off to the small garrison mess, only to find all the officers away at a practice camp. However, I was given an excellent dinner. It was a hot moonlit night and a great change to the train, so I found a gharri to drive me around the cantonments. The driver drove me towards the large Indian town, where there was a huge pro-Gandhi demonstration with the usual hundreds of yelling Indians. About fifty youths surrounded the gharri. I didn't much like the look of them, so I lifted the driver down on to the back seat and took his place, very quickly arriving back in the cantonments at a gallop. There the whole place was bristling with men of a British infantry battalion. How happy I would have been to have been stationed there, a single battery station and the finest pig-sticking in India. After an excellent early breakfast in the mess, I drove back to the station where, to my amazement, my now much refreshed companion arrived. A proper bath, food, medicine and an excellent night had done wonders. At long last we reached Bombay with the P&O ship in the harbour. I explained everything to the ship's doctor who was not at all keen on allowing her on board; however with her mother dying in England he agreed and made her very comfortable in the sick bay. She was in tears when she kissed me passionately and very sweetly good-bye. I never saw her again. She wrote me a charming letter some months later. If she is alive today, I am quite sure she is as sweet and as beautiful as she was then.

I got back to Kirkee where no one was in the least interested where I had been. Another officer had been allotted my bungalow and all the cats were back in the mess. The adjutant told me to collect my belongings and set off for Secunderabad in the centre of the Deccan to join the 34th Battery. My bearer turned up, delighted to see me and took charge of everything. I called on the colonel and set off, quite happy to leave.

Chapter 4

SECUNDERABAD

The Nizam, the absolute ruler of a vast state, lived in his palace at Hyderabad, a very large and crowded city, on the banks of the Musi river. He was not a pleasant looking man, though an extremely efficient ruler. A miser of the first order, he had collected a very large treasure in jewels and gold ingots. He also collected concubines in his efforts to produce a son. Secunderabad and the cantonments, which stretched for some twelve miles, had excellent barracks of double storied bungalows, with deep verandahs and a view for miles. A very pleasant station, with a cavalry brigade, an infantry brigade, a horse artillery battery and a field battery, surrounded by vast plains, dotted with palm trees. Here I stayed for five years and I thoroughly enjoyed every day. Sinclair, my brother subaltern, became a life-long friend.

We were fortunate in having 'I' Battery Royal Horse Artillery with us – probably the smartest and most efficient unit in the British army at that time. All the officers, much decorated, had been together for several years. I envied them and became much attached to all of them. Except during the rains, we paraded at 6.30 a.m. every morning and rode off with our guns across the plains. All great fun! Then back to breakfast, musketry, signalling and other boring jobs until stables. The men were young and much enjoyed the life. I got to know them well. I learnt to play polo and managed to purchase progressively better ponies. I taught my charger to show-jump up to a very modest standard.

The small game shooting was average but you had to work hard for it; plenty of black buck, with their lovely spiral horns on the plains and the chinkara in the hills. I discovered that a small metre-gauge train set off once a week from Hyderabad on a Wednesday night. Now Thursday was a holiday in India, so that if the gods were willing, a nice long weekend could be had. This enlarged my hunting area enormously.

My Indian orderly, who had soon contacted me, set off two or three days earlier, with a bullock cart, a horse for me and my hog-spear. He set up the camp, and my bearer and I followed, arriving in the dawn. Here were the zemindaries on the fringe of the protected jungle, with the beautiful spotted deer in abundance and always the chance of a big boar in the early dawn or a leopard in the dusk, maybe a sloth-bear, a dangerous and unpredictable animal.

I read every book I could find about hunting big game in India and was slowly acquiring knowledge and common sense. Sadly I was madly impatient and I am sure I missed many a good chance through this. I found the village shikaris most helpful and I grew to love the forest people. Looking back today, I fancy I was in their eyes only a 'little Bahadur', not a Barragh Sahib from whom a great reward could be expected!

Back in the cantonments the rains came, when everything shut down, and then the cold weather, with manoeuvres and camping out for a month or so. Great fun with wonderful sand grouse shooting, duck and sometimes a goose on off days. Could a man ask for more? Oh yes, for this cold weather brought out the charming sisters and cousins of the wives of the Indian cavalry officers. I had more friends in the Deccan Horse than in either of the other two cavalry regiments and naturally paired off with one of their most attractive sisters. We did everything together for two months, then she went off to Delhi or Calcutta for Christmas week and I never saw her again. This happened every year but I must admit that in my last Christmas at Secunderabad, I did brood over my Nephite, though I did meet her again once in London.

Spring of 1924 came and most of the leaves fell off the trees, leaving the tinsmith birds and the maddening brain-fever birds to sing their hideous songs. I was ordered to attend a banquet given by Sir Asfar-el-Mulk, the commander-in-chief of the Nizam's army, in his palace at Hyderabad. He was a very fine old man and had been with General Roberts at Kandahar. He was under the wing of the British Government so the Nizam could not banish him or steal all his property, as was his wont. We sat down at a huge table, about eighty to a hundred, men only, eating off very fine and very dirty silver plates and waited on by an army of retainers in the remains of ancient uniforms, plus curved swords. It went on for hours, curries, pilaffs and very good fruit. I was so tired, I slept on the roadside on my way home.

Ludo Graham of 'I' Battery and I ran the race course. We had several meetings and very reasonable racing. The most popular race was the Secunderabad Polo Pony Scurry, owners up. All the officers of the 9th Lancers backed their English bred ponies heavily, so did everyone else. There was a Selling Sweepstake, the winner scooped the lot. My pony was quite unplayable at polo, as it frequently left the polo ground. However, I won the race with ease and received a large silver cup and two thousand rupees.

The Rajput Regiment whose cantonments were nearest to Hyderabad, invited a large number of officers and their wives to a moonlight picnic at Golconda Fort. This magnificent fort had in times gone by been the last stronghold of the Hindus of the Deccan in the face of the Mogul invasion. They retired into their stronghold with all their wealth, gold and jewels, their wives, concubines and retainers. They withheld every onslaught for months then the water gave out, a traitor opened a postern door and the Muslims poured in. The

Hindus fought until the last man was killed, then all the wives, concubines and servants leapt from the battlements to their death, which they preferred to being ravished by the Muslims. For years men have searched for the immense treasure hidden in its walls; some of it must have been discovered for the famous Golconda Diamond is in one of Her Majesty's crowns today.

It was full moon and as light as day. After a marvellous supper, we all trooped into the fort, an old Buddhist priest with a lantern leading us. In a few minutes everyone split up and disappeared which was quite usual in moonlight picnics! Sometime later I was surveying the countryside from the top battlements, thinking of the Hindu warriors that night so many years ago, when a woman appeared from a pitch dark staircase, clutching hold of me saying, 'I am so frightened, I cannot speak. I was left alone down there in the dark, please don't leave me.' I was scared too, not so much by the imagined groans of the dying Hindu warriors, or the screams of their women but of the snakes which I knew must be living all over the fort. It took us quite a time to find our way down to the gateway and then everybody was around, mounting their horses and setting off for home.

Her husband was the regimental orderly officer and so had had to remain behind. I was dead beat after two and a half hours ride, when we reached their bungalow. She gave me a mattress on their verandah and I was asleep in a moment. Over breakfast, her husband thought the whole thing very funny, but neither she nor I laughed.

Dotted about the plains of the Deccan and indeed in most of Southern India are the most extraordinary occasional piles of gigantic volcanic rock, maybe sixty to eighty feet high. It is among these rocks that the leopards or panthers live, and sally forth to prey on the flocks and herds of the villagers. The panther is the most beautiful, the cruellest and the most dangerous of all the animals of the Indian jungle. I never shot at one unless I was absolutely certain of killing it stone dead. To have to follow up a wounded panther is a horrifying job. To one of my camps in the Deccan, a European was brought in; he had been badly mauled by a wounded panther, his arm was enormously swollen and had turned gangrenous. The smell was awful. I should have taken his arm off, but as I had no saw, I would have been compelled to use an axe, and in those days I was not all that tough. I did slit the arm all the way down with my hunting knife. He had five days to go in a bullock cart, but he made it and survived. He was very fortunate.

After lunch one very hot day, I found a villager sitting on my verandah. I was told he had walked many miles to ask me to return with him and shoot a very large panther that was decimating the village flocks. Not all these tales are true, but he seemed genuine enough, so we set off, my orderly and I. We rode about ten miles and arrived at his village as evening was approaching. Sure enough there was a huge pile of rocks, the village below it, and he pointed out a large flat rock, where he said the panther sat every evening. The village fires were just being lit and their smoke mingled with the dust from the returning flocks turned pink as the sun set.

Suddenly there was the panther, a very large male surveying his prospective kill. I shot at once and, hitting him through the heart, killed him instantly. He was my first panther and I was thrilled; he measured nine feet. The whole village turned out as he was brought down on a pole and put into a bullock cart for the journey home. His skin is in my dressing room today, so many miles from where he lived and so many years since he died.

From then on I made this animal my main preoccupation, sitting up for them on lonely rocks in the evening and at full moon. I even shot a beautiful female in the middle of a village. There were many disappointing hunts but over the years I shot some lovely animals. Only once was I stupid: in thick jungle, I shot a very young cub by mistake and, had the mother been a trifle more courageous, she would have killed me.

India 1924

Near the Nizam's palace on the northern outskirts of the native city of Hyderabad stood a charming and beautiful small residence, the original home of the British Resident. Here a guard of one officer and fifty other ranks were permanently housed, each regiment in turn supplying the men for this most unpopular duty of ten days duration. Communication was by heliograph from the roof at dawn and at dusk. Now it was my turn to do duty there. The native city was out of bounds thank goodness. I explored the extensive and very beautiful garden where I discovered a small marble replica of the residency. I enquired about this and was told that, at the turn of the century, the then resident fell in love with a beautiful Hindu princess. While he was in England on his leave, she had the replica made and in the evening she put candles inside and longed for his return. She was sixteen and very much in love. He returned in due course, bringing an English wife with him. That evening the princess went out into the garden and hung herself in a young tree nearby. From that day to this, that tree has never shed its leaves or grown any older. They say whoever sees the marble replica lit up at night is dead by the morning.

I had nothing to do, so I rode over to visit the Nizam's cavalry – the Halisicka Lancers. They were a very efficient body of cut-throats with gorgeous uniforms and sturdy country-bred horses. I met the Nizam's prime minister at lunch there. He also had nothing to do as the Nizam had banished him to one of his country estates, but as his job was hereditary it could not be for long. His palace was a series of charming courtyards, on the ground floor all the rooms were completely bare. This, he explained, was in case the Nizam visited him and showed approval of any object, which he then had to present to him.

The prime minister's father had collected swords, hundreds and hundreds of them, while he himself had collected walking sticks while at Cambridge. Neither of his two Rolls Royces would run. I think he thought I could do something about them but I couldn't. We finally decided to go and hunt the Nizam's famous herd of black buck. We shot a good one and then had to gallop for our lives.

My tour of duty over, I returned to my battery and somewhat prosaic soldiering. Musketry was the order of the day; my young soldiers were the worst shots in India. However, this suited me as every day for two months I was in charge of the rifle ranges. I was determined to become an army marksman, no easy achievement, and fired hundreds of rounds. I knew it might be crucial to me when hunting one day. I was no wiser in the art of gunnery.

The bubonic plague hit the city of Hyderabad. No one was allowed out of the cantonments; when the dead reached a thousand a week, the Nizam decided to burn down one third of the city, lying in a loop of the river, and asked for British assistance.

We were all scared stiff, but we had to take our turn. The fires raged for three weeks, burning thousands of rats and probably hundreds of very old Indians. The rats which swam the river were killed on the far bank by the Nizam's army. The plague died away; only two British soldiers caught it and, of course, died, as did the dedicated doctor and nurse who tended them. Bubonic plague is the worst of all the Indian epidemics.

Every evening I spent hours poring over maps and trying to decide for which forest blocks to apply for my next two months hot weather leave. I did not find any of the forest officers in the least helpful. I only wanted tigers and there were plenty of them. I tried blocks of forest in the United Provinces, the Central

Provinces, the Deccan and east to Orissa. Of course I shot antelopes to eat and feed the jungle people, a few snipe and duck, bison if I could find one, panthers and sloth bears, but I kept the forest as quiet as I could. I spent night after night at the full moon sitting up a tree waiting for a nice large tiger to come and eat a small calf which I had tethered below but not one ever came. Yet, walking back to my camp one morning, I passed the village jeel or pond, where, splashing about and having a lovely time, was a fair sized tiger which I had been hunting for two weeks. To try a shot I thought was too risky and too near the village; maybe I was wrong.

When trekking across the Deccan in 1925, into the Chandra State, I spent a night in a border village, which was dominated by a huge ruffian of an Indian. He gave me palm tree toddy, hoping no doubt to make me insensible and then steal my rifle. We were sitting in a charming courtyard with hundreds of white doves. He was a great tiger hunter and had built a strong cage with a trap door, with a compartment sealed off for a small bullock as bait – the whole thing on huge wooden wheels. An avaricious little Indian was bribed to sit on top in order to release the door as the tiger entered. Needless to say it was the Indian that the tiger always ate. He offered the role of the Indian to me, which I refused, so he produced a bullock cart with a magnificent pair of white bullocks. The plan was to drive at speed through the forest in the hopes that a very hungry tiger would attack the bullocks and I could then shoot it. The result of course was absolutely nothing.

Owing to the great heat, my two bullock carts and I trekked all night at a steady two miles an hour and then rested most of the day. There was no moon but the brilliance of the stars helped us see our way. The jungle around us was never still or silent – small herds of deer moving to a waterhole, a leopard attacking them, sounds of wild pig hurrying past, monkeys chattering in terror at a tree snake, then with the dawn approaching the scream of a peacock and another day had come.

Back at home at Secunderabad, I would walk into the mess and probably Peter Percival would look up and say, 'Look who is here, some poor tiger has missed a good meal.'

One autumn on manoeuvres, we ventured south into the Mahratta country. This was quite unlike any other part of India, wild hilly rocky terrain, inhabited by wild very brave tribes.

My orderly and I were riding back to camp one evening; we both had hog spears and I had my two large Rampur hounds with me and glad I was to have them.

We rode through a narrow valley, past a dozen grass huts or so and a few cooking fires. In a moment we were both surrounded by a bevy of beautiful women and girls, their hair curling over their shoulders, flashing teeth, sparkling eyes and gaily coloured bodices with flowing skirts. They tried to pull us off our horses. Their arms and legs were covered with large silver bangles, for they owned no land. They were Gonds and they lived by terrorising the villagers. Their menfolk were strong, sturdy and sullen. Of the two, I fancy the women were the more deadly but they bore us no ill will and called repeatedly as we cantered away. I was glad to put several miles behind us before we reached camp.

In 1926 I planned to join Frank Spurrell in Tanganyika for my leave, so my choice of forest blocks for the hot weather of 1925 was crucial. I must kill a tiger there.

I chose a forest in Orissa. I knew nothing about the country, though I did know that very few Europeans went there. The local people appeared to be temperamental. Captain Bazelleget, whom I had known well in England, was stoned to death on the steps of his court house a couple of months before I went there, over some agricultural grievance.

Orissa was a very hot place in May and dry as a bone. I had about five miles to walk across country to find my camp. As I walked along the sandy path, I noticed continual marks of snakes crossing the path. I idly asked my guide, 'What happens to a man who is bitten by one of these snakes?'

'Sahib, they die. Some die slowly, some die quickly but they all die.' I was to remember this some days later.

There was only one huge pepul tree slap in the middle of a small village. The headman invited me to pitch my tent in its shade and demolished a hut to give me room. Next evening I gave the villagers a feast and told them I wanted to shoot a tiger. They were not in the least interested and said no-one had entered the adjoining forest for some months and there was certainly no tiger living there. For two weeks I scoured the forest block allotted to me. I shot an occasional sambhur for the villagers in the open forest glades but found no pug marks of leopard, tiger or sloth bears. The village hunter was an intelligent old man. He said, 'Wait, sahib, all the animals have not yet returned. Some weeks ago, a pack of wild dogs, the red dole of the Deccan, came into the forest and they drove every living animal far, far away, but they will return.' He then took me to a deep ravine with huge rocks lying about and thick bushes and jungle, a very sinister, silent place, with myriads of white butterflies and heavily scented with frangipani. I took an instant dislike to the place. However there was a small deep pool, in a fissure of rock, a small tree beside it. I decided to sit up in that tree that night and see who came to drink. I duly sent the old man home and climbed into the tree. As evening approached the pool became alive with snakes. To my horror a long green tree snake had climbed up my tree to dry out. In a flash I was down and running flat out the couple of miles to my camp, for there was no moon and I did not like snakes.

Two weeks later the moon was full and my old shikari showed me a thick tree full of fruit, not far from the ravine in completely open country. Two game trails crossed fifty yards away. He said, 'Sahib, you and I will sit up in that tree tonight. Many sloth-bear will come out of the ravine to eat the fruit.' Towards evening as I was collecting my rifle and a shot gun, a message was brought to me that the old shikari was laid low with fever and that his son would accompany me. The son duly arrived. I did not take to him and he smelt abominably. However I had to have someone to carry my second gun. We got to the tree before dark and settled ourselves most uncomfortably as high as we could.

The full moon rose and it was as light as day but of course pitch dark in the shadow of the tree. Without a sound the bears arrived. I never saw one, but soon the tree was full of them. Now sloth-bears are dangerous and unpredictable and as I did not fancy one or two on my bough, I fired a shot with my 12-bore. The effect was terrific; about a dozen bears dropped to the ground, nearly taking me with them and dashed away. I thought they wouldn't come back that night and settled myself to sleep.

A few hours later, I distinctly heard the voice of my old shikari saying, 'Sahib, sahib, sher hi, the tiger is here.' I knew he was back in his village and his worthless son was fast asleep above me. It was absolutely quiet and I could see no animal anywhere. As soon as it was getting light, I got down and inspected the game track and there not fifty yards from the tree were the pugmarks of a full sized tiger. At that moment, a sambhur sounded his alarm note or bell, so I walked noiselessly along the narrow game trail leading to the dense jungle around the ravine. Suddenly in front of me, I saw the tiger walking along ahead of me, swinging his tail. He stopped and half turned to look back. I knew he had neither winded nor seen me and then I took a very careful shot. He gave one roar and then there was dead silence. What I had done was the most stupid and senseless thing an experienced hunter could do. Undoubtedly the tiger was wounded but how badly, it was impossible to tell. My rifle was a .375 Männlicher. Very slowly I walked backwards to the edge of the thick jungle, picked up my 12-bore gun, dropped by my worthless gun bearer as he fled for his life, and I returned to my camp in the village.

There I despatched a runner to the nearest forest officer. I ate a large breakfast and instructed the headman of the village to round up all the village water buffaloes. In the afternoon the forest officer, an Indian, arrived. We then returned to the spot where I had shot the tiger and drove the buffaloes back and forth. The theory is that when they scent blood they put their heads together and charge forward. In fact they did nothing but eat leaves and berries, while we peered about very nervously. There was very little blood to be found. It was a dreadful place, large rocks covered with creepers and thick bushes. The forest officer thought that the tiger dragged himself back into the ravine where to follow him would be to invite disaster. Not a villager would come with me even to within half a mile of the place and I did at least have the common sense not to go in alone and search round again. Thus ended for me my efforts at killing a tiger. I had been a fool and I knew it. I only had a day or two left before my tenancy of the forest block expired.

In fact when his remains were found some days later, he had only moved a few feet and must have been lying dead as we milled around. The shot had missed the heart by half an inch, smashing both shoulders. The forest officer who wrote all this to me said his skin when discovered was ruined by putrefaction. I wonder how true this was, for anyway the head should have been mountable.

When I got back to Secunderabad, the rains started and everything closed down. I had to give my poor soldiers a lecture every day on some inane subject and then we took one of the 13-pounder guns to pieces and next day put it together again.

Chapter 5

THE EQUITATION SCHOOL, SAUGOR

I had a couple of new polo ponies to school in the fine movements but I made no attempt to shoot anything. Early in August I was told that I had been selected to go to the Equitation School at Saugor on a nine months course. I was simply delighted. The aim of the course was to instruct regimental officers how to train the remounts allotted to their regiments annually. Most of the officers were British Indian cavalrymen and a more charming lot of young men it would be hard to find. I made a lot of very good friends. For them the course was a farce as all their remounts were trained annually by their own non-commissioned havildhars, so they just played polo and very well too. There were a few pleasant gunners and a couple of British cavalrymen. The instructors were the very best. From the day I arrived at Saugor I enjoyed every moment of every day. The remount I was given proved untrainable and, having nearly killed two men, was shot and I was given another, not much better.

I went off shooting in the open jungles nearby most weekends and found them inhabited by the beautiful spotted deer called cheetal. I managed to kill a few leopard and a lot of dreadful crocodiles. As Christmas approached and the grass died down, pig-sticking started. Many books have been written on this subject so I won't even start to describe the sport, only to comment that it is, bar none, the most exciting and dangerous mounted sport in the world. Mrs Vigors, the attractive wife of the second in command, used to ride in our heats and she neither asked nor gave an inch to any of us, killing a more than average number of fierce old boars to her spear. A pig-sticking camp embodies all the best that an Indian winter can provide, all the horses on their lines, the big fires at night and the chilly hunt each dawn with the best company in the world.

There were only five women at the equitation school and they had sixty pretty ardent young men to deal with, which they accomplished with a pleasant skill. I made friends with a tall dark young woman. She was the wife of the district divisional police commissioner and consequently had to be treated with decorum. She told me the story of the gunner major who lived in their bungalow just before the 1914 war. One evening at a guest night, he was holding forth that there was nothing a gunner could not do. A cavalryman took him up, laid fifty

Polo at Saugor

rupees on the table and said, 'I bet you and your gunners could not get two of your guns to the top of that steep hill by dawn.' The major, now thoroughly sobered up, went back to his battery and told them of his bet. They were mad keen and every man turned out. They toiled all night and fashioned a track round and round that very steep hill. Just before the sun rose, as it was lightening in the east, the first gun and gun team galloped up to the top. The second one followed closely behind, but the track gave way and down the gun team went; horses and drivers, all were killed. The major mounted his horse and rode home to his bungalow. He was still in scarlet mess kit and as he mounted the steps of the verandah, his spurs jingled. Arrived in his room, he shot himself. My friend told me that they often heard the footsteps of this gunner major but had never seen his ghost.

She and I rode up to the top of that hill one morning as the sun rose and, though the view was marvellous, we both felt for the death of those men and horses not so long ago.

As the course neared its end, we had all sorts of competitions, including a sixty-mile long ride carrying sixteen stone and ending up with one circuit of the steeplechase course, no spurs or whip. A tremendously exciting race meeting, every race a battle. I was lucky and won two steeplechases and a flat race. Then all the first class polo players went off to Meerut for the Inter Regimental Polo Tournament.

Gradually we sorted ourselves out; I sold all my horses and sadly said goodbye to my many friends, none of whom I ever saw again. One evening I rode over to the native city of Saugor, about five or six miles away. I was immensely interested in the famous fort where two thousand mutineers held out against the two Irregular Cavalry Regiments, Skinners and Probyns Horse. Having captured the fort, they hung every man left alive, but as they had no rope, each mutineer had to make a rope out of his own clothes.

A man I would very much like to see again was a Rajput prince. He often invited me to shoot at weekends. He only flew his falcons while I shot partridge or anything that turned up. In the evenings in his comfortable camp, every man sat down at the same long table, for they were all Rajputs and their rank and caste were the same.

Chris Birdwood asked me to go with him to the Maharajah of Baroda's imperial sand grouse shoot, which the maharajah arranged annually for the viceroy. His palace of white marble was built alongside a lake, with many islands on several of which were small marble guest houses. In one of these, Chris and I were housed. It was a setting out of this world. Thousands of sand grouse came in to drink at the lake side in the morning. For me it was a complete farce as I only had fifty 12-bore cartridges. The tiger shoot next day was even worse; the four tigers were driven very cleverly to each of the three important guests and of course the maharajah. I would have had a much better chance of killing one up a tree in Regents Park.

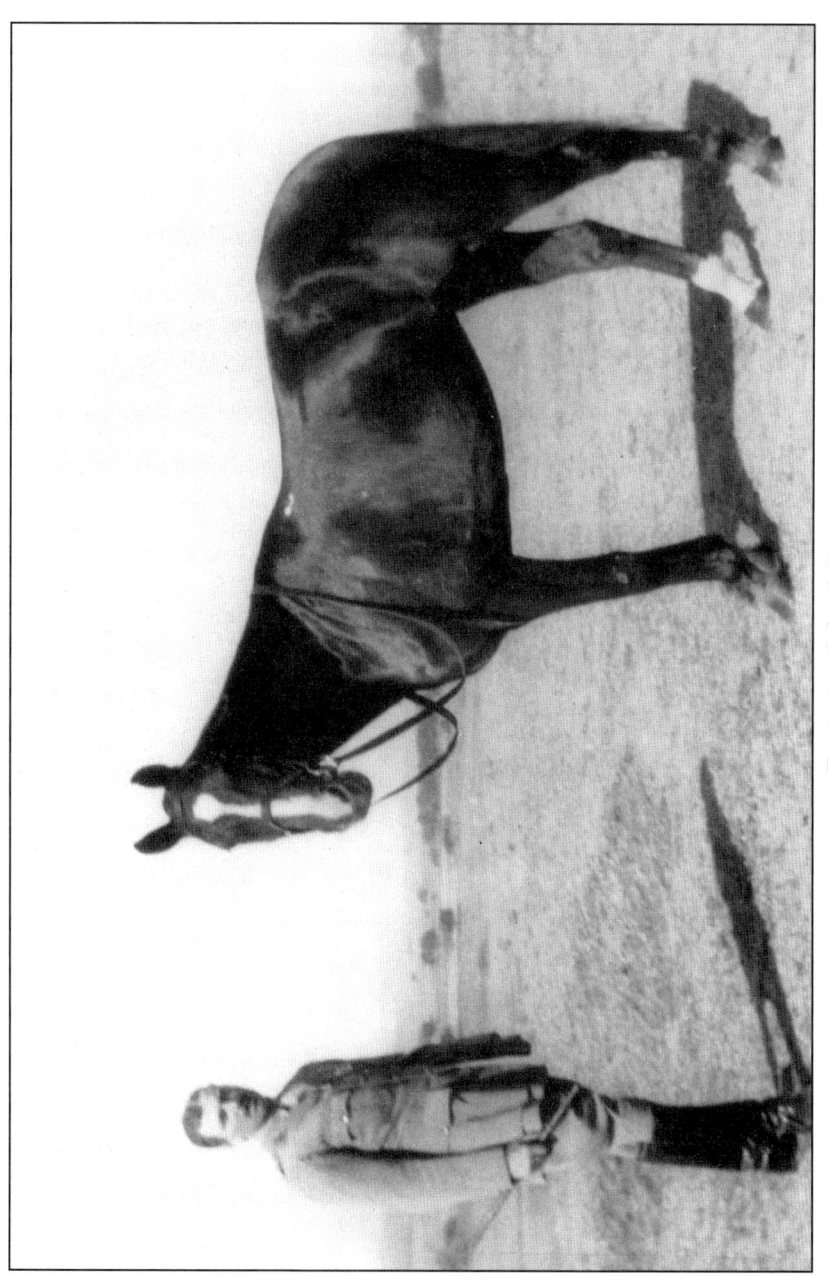

Equitation School, Saugor

Chris and I then travelled up to Goona, the hereditary station of the Guides Cavalry, where we spent a very pleasant few days, shooting and pig sticking. There were deep depressions of several hundred square miles, every now and then. Here the jungles were thick and we had a drive for tiger, which abounded, but the grass was still much too high. A tigress and her four delightful cubs walked under my tree, I could not get a reasonable shot, so I let her go in peace.

On my return to my battery, I was told to take my two months leave, so I sent a wire to Frank Spurrell, telling him I hoped to be with him in his Masai reserve in Tanganyika shortly.

Just as I was leaving, a little babu or Indian office clerk came to see me. He said, 'Sahib, you took six horses to Saugor as allowed by regulations and government paid their rail fare. Now you have returned but you have not applied for the return fare of the six horses. This money is owed to you and until I receive your application I cannot pay you the money and therefore I cannot make my book correct.'

I tried to explain that I had sold all my six horses. This he would not believe and said, 'Sahib, you took six horses with you; now I know British officers do not eat their horses, nor can horses fly, therefore six horses must have returned from Saugor. Please sign this application so that I can pay you the money and my book will be correct.'

Weakly, I gave up and signed; the little babu was delighted.

Chapter 6

THE MASAI RESERVE, TANGANYIKA

I had known Frank Spurrell for many years; he was my best friend, an excellent shot and he lived in Norfolk. I was much in love with his sister Margaret, but it happened that we did not marry. When Frank went out to Tanganyika our plan was for him to visit me in India and hunt a tiger and for me to visit him and hunt a lion. So I set off from Bombay in a small steamer, the Karoa. What I did not know was that the Karoa was completely unseaworthy and due to go to the bottom of the sea at any moment. Nor did I know that the month of June was a very bad time to cross the Indian Ocean on account of cyclones.

My companions were a nice looking woman from Java, who had become an opium addict, a completely silent British officer of an Indian infantry regiment, and a tall dark woman who had been ordered out of Shanghai. After several pleasant days sailing, a storm hit us the like of which I had never imagined possible. The deck was permanently awash and the sea poured in everywhere. We moved up into the smoking room and settled down there. The woman from Java had her fascinating opium laid out. The Indian infantry officer stayed on deck; I think he was only semi-conscious and just floated about. I roped him several times to stanchions and got very wet doing so. Inevitably he went over the side sometime during the night. The purser joined us and we drank a lot of whisky; a mixture of that and the opium finished me, I passed out. On coming to, I found the ship stationary in a flat calm sea. The first officer ordered us into a partially filled life-boat attached by a long rope to the bow of the ship, the object being to turn us away from the African shore. We spent a couple of rather hot uncomfortable days just sitting put and trying to make the woman from Java stop wailing at the loss of her opium pipe.

At long last the steering gear was partially repaired and we crept into Mombasa harbour. I leapt ashore and sat about on good firm land until a train set off for the interior in the evening. The woman from Shanghai followed me and went off in a rage when I flatly refused to give her £20. The train stopped at a small station called Voi, which was pitch dark with marvellous stars above. I unrolled my bedding and slept like a log until dawn, when a charming man woke me up with a huge mug of coffee. He said his name was Swinerton and that we would travel together to Arusha on the monthly water train. This consisted of a small engine fuelled by wood and a long line of trucks each containing a tank of water.

At each halt we dropped off a truck. I was very interested in Tsavo, a famous place for lion. The railway line finished at Moshi and Swinerton took me on in one of his trucks, dropping me at the officers' mess of the Kenya African Rifles Regiment. I liked him immensely; he told me he was the government tsetse fly officer and that we might well meet at Frank Spurrell's kraal.

The KARR mess was delightful, a lovely garden full of trees and flowers. The officers could not have been kinder. The mess was perched high up on the side of Mount Meru and looked out over the plains below. As there was no train south for a week, one of the officers suggested that we took a truck and went down to the plains to try and shoot a couple of good oryx antelopes. They are lovely creatures with long, very sharp horns; no lion will attack them. We shot two beautiful oryx and several Grant and Thompson gazelles, then unfortunately my companion developed pneumonia and was very ill. We contacted the mess high above us by heliograph and the medical officer came down in a truck next morning and drove us back.

Frank Spurrell was the District Officer of a huge area of the Masai Reserve. He had sent me a photograph of his HQ. This consisted of five rondel huts, a flag staff, a medical orderly and a horrible young ostrich. The Masai tribe, the most interesting in all Africa, erupted from maybe the Southern Sudan, at that time fertile grassland, about a thousand years ago. The tribe, in the course of time, spread south for some two thousand miles. They followed the line the elephants had taken, using their water holes, keeping to the dry bush country, killing every living soul of any tribe they met. Eventually they occupied this enormous area, with their warriors and young girls in small kraals, their married older men, their wives and huge herds of very poor cattle in a central kraal near a water hole. They have no language. I have never heard one speak. They do no manual work, they grow no crops and it seemed to me that the women lived on milk and the warriors and young girls lived on what they could find in the bush. The whole tribe was very strictly controlled by a chosen group of elders, who lived somewhere on Mount Meru. When a boy reached the age of 16 or 17, each one made his own way to Mount Meru, where he underwent initiation ceremonies, finally receiving his nine foot spear. He became a warrior or Moran, painting himself all over with red ochre which he never washed off. They are instinctively very brave, they will surround and kill a lion in the open bush with their spears.

With reluctance I said goodbye to the officers of the KARR and travelled south on the weekly train. At breakfast I met a white hunter named Reels; he had been bitten by a bug which rendered him completely blind for six months. He gave me a great deal of useful advice when dealing with rhino, which he said abounded in the district I hoped to reach. My other companion was a young schoolteacher from Tanga. Immediately we became friends. He told me that if I ever reached Tanga, to send him a wire and he would arrange for me to shoot a sable antelope. This in fact he did months later.

We arrived at a halt called Hedaru. I left the train and looked around for Frank but not a soul was in sight. The little Indian stationmaster approached me and listened to what I had to say. 'Well, sahib, your friend will certainly not come to Hedaru. No-one has travelled the road from Kibaya for the last three years. No matter, I will see what can be done for I certainly do not want you here for many days.' There was a store nearby run by two young Germans, where I had an excellent meal. The stationmaster then re-appeared with a young man who said he had an open truck and he would take me the two hundred miles, if we could get there, for £20! I bought what provisions I thought we needed, he got a couple of tins of water and we set off. It was a lovely day, the rough track ran due south across the bush. Progress was slow, most of the bridges across the dry nullahs were broken down so we had to dig away the bank to get down and up the other side. We slept in the truck and set off again at sunrise. About mid-day we suddenly saw four magnificent greater kudu with their huge spiral horns. I jumped out of the truck with my rifle and set off after them. They had of course disappeared. I never saw greater kudu again in Africa. I was completely lost. I fired a shot but heard no shout from the driver. I could not believe it but there was no track and no truck visible. I looked up and there almost beside me was an extraordinary figure, a young man about six feet six inches tall, completely naked, except for a loose cloth knotted over one shoulder. He was standing on one leg, leaning on a huge spear, the other leg bent on to his knee and painted all over with red ochre. My words of greeting were completely ignored. He turned and walked off in the opposite direction. I followed and in a very few minutes there was the truck and we both climbed into the back.

You may well believe in many things that I do not but I do not believe that that Masai warrior was standing there by chance, for there were no Masai kraals for a hundred miles or more. We made good progress that day, saw no more game of any sort and were just settling down for the night, when I saw a light about a mile away. The driver said it could not be real, so I urged him to light a small fire nearby and I would walk over and see what it was. It turned out to be the camp of a company of KARR trekking north to Arusha. They had been trekking for three months and had still far to go. We spent the night with them very pleasantly.

We reached Kibaya safely, where Frank was delighted to see me, not noticeably changed at all. He showed me an empty rondel hut, empty except for the ostrich, to settle down in. He wasn't in the least surprised to see me, for he said four sons of various Masai chiefs had arrived a few weeks ago to await my arrival. All this I found very queer.

Kibaya could not have been a more lonely spot, miles and miles from

Tanganyika Territory

anywhere. In daylight I found Africa a pleasant place, but by night it was very different, then a cruel, hostile country and absolutely silent.

Frank told me that he was leaving in two days time, when his supplies arrived by ox-train from Kondoa, to rejoin some four hundred Swahili natives with whom he was clearing a track twelve feet wide running due east, presumably to open up the country for well-diggers who were due that winter. Water was very scarce and the Masai cattle were dying fast. The ox-train duly arrived, two huge wagons each drawn by eight pairs of black oxen and off we set. Frank had done all the big game shooting he wanted when he had first arrived in Africa and I found his advice was excellent. He said never follow a wounded dangerous animal, either shoot it dead or leave it alone. It was a waste of time to shoot lion as there was no means of preserving the skin, rhino he strongly advised leaving alone, also buffalo, which were most dangerous. He allotted me a Dorobo hunter and excellent tracker, and the job of shooting game to feed his men.

There were herds and herds of antelope, from the lovely impala to the hideous wildebeest, giraffe, zebra, ostrich and many more species, also of course many lions. We got up at dawn every morning, he organised his men, sending off a small party to make the next night's camp and find water, probably eight to ten miles away. I scouted around with my excellent little Dorobo tracker who was only about 4 feet 10 inches high and spoke little or nothing, also my four chiefs' sons who just walked along about four hundred yards behind us. The Dorobo hunters are tolerated by the Masai because they recognise the honey-birds who lead them to a wild bees' hive, probably in a hole of an old tree. The Masai then burn the tree down and fall on the honey-comb, which was the only thing they were really enthusiastic about. About four o'clock the new camp fire was lit with a curl of smoke and Frank and I converged on it. I then shot what game was needed for the men that night as near the camp as possible and awaited the four long lines of Swahili coming in. Each long line had its singer, who kept them going, every man joining in the chorus. I imagine this was to keep off the lions. It was all highly romantic.

One morning I was limping along talking to Frank. I had been bitten by a jigger under my toe-nail and now had to wait until its eggs turned into maggots before cutting them out, when around a thorn tree walked a very pleasant sight. Four absolutely stark naked Masai girls, nice and plump with comely figures and breasts, but not a single hair on their heads or bodies. Like the serowe in the far off Himalayas, they were frozen in their tracks at the sight of us, then gone in a flash. For the next couple of miles, bunches of them kept appearing and disappearing.

Soon we came to a water hole; the water was about twenty-five feet down and plenty of it. A cutting ran down to the water probably scooped out by an elephant at some ancient time. Each cow in the vast herds had to walk through this tunnel to drink. It seemed to me lunatic that the Masai had never thought of lifting the water up in gourds and then into a trough. But then they were set against any form of manual labour.

The old men offered us milk, which was very welcome and asked us to stay in their kraal. Their huts were primitive beyond words, the flies were appalling and their wives, several of whom they allotted to us, were a truly awe-inspiring sight. Shaven heads, sagging breasts and covered with untanned cow-hide. Of course all the cows were herded in every night against the attacks of lion, the whole kraal being surrounded by a ten feet high hedge of thorn bushes with spikes six inches long. Lions frequently leapt into the kraal and stampeded the cattle. We firmly declined all their kind offers and we intimated to them that we would have their water hole vastly improved. In return they asked us to stay nearby for a day or two.

A couple of days later, twenty elders took us to a small hill and as we waited I could hear a curious dull murmuring. Then without warning there appeared about five hundred warriors or Moran in their full battle array, huge ostrich feather head-dresses, completely naked with every bone in their body coloured white by wood ash, each man carried his spear and large white hide striped shields. They circled round us and appeared to me very frightening. I was delighted to see them go. The whole episode reminded me of what the Zulus must have looked like at Rorke's Drift.

My foot completely healed up and I went hunting again every morning, always exciting as one never knew what would turn up. My Dorobo suddenly became very animated, jumping up and down as he drew my attention by hitting me hard with his sheathed hunting sword. I could see nothing unusual but on approaching a dense thicket, I saw at least twenty very large beasts. The largest bull was immense and had short very thick ribbed horns. I shot him and also another one in my excitement. They all disappeared, even my Dorobo. I raced round the thicket and fell into a pit someone had dug for an elephant. By the time I had clambered out, I got a fleeting glimpse of a pride of lions, about nine of them, tearing away and I could hear my Dorobo chanting in the thicket. I found him standing on the great bull singing the theme reserved for the death of a truly great beast. So it turned out to be – a giant eland and a Rowland Ward record.

We cut up the beasts and, as the lions were all around, we decided to stay the night in a tree there and keep them off the carcasses. In this we were only partially successful as they ate the whole of the smaller bull and frightened us all night.

Our one bugbear in the bush was the rhino. Each rhino walks along and makes his own path, placing each foot exactly in front of the other, making a trough eight inches wide and four inches deep, quite impossible for a European to follow. When he has eaten his fill, he goes off and stands behind a thick thorn tree, alongside his path. There he spends the heat of the day and if you happen to pass by, he suddenly scents this very offensive smell emanating from you, immediately dashes out, gallops along his path, four tons at about thirty miles an hour. You have no time to do anything except throw yourself into a thorn bush with spikes at least six inches long. This happens several times every day. Rhinos are peaceful creatures and, except for their sense of smell, are really quite harmless. But they are almost impossible to shoot, and quite worthless if you did shoot them, because I personally was not interested in their horn which to some people is of great value.

Our Swahilis needed plenty of water and Frank was getting more and more worried about the water-holes. They were few and far between and they were very hard to find. The Masai were completely useless, they would not even go and look for them. One evening we were making do with a deep but very small water-hole. For some reason I made our cook boil enough water for my water bottle and a long gourd which we tried always to keep full, for ourselves. The night was very dark.

In the early morning when I awoke, I smelt a very familiar warm smell, and there not six feet from my head was a huge pile of steaming elephant dung, a sight to warm the heart of every African hunter. I woke Frank and we looked with amazement at the size of the footmarks, they were immense. There was nothing left of the waterhole, the elephant had sucked it almost dry and then urinated into it. Of course I was mad keen to go after this huge lone bull. To shoot an elephant, if you obey the rules, is easy and a highly stupid thing to do, for he is a marvellous animal, very wise and exceedingly clever. When he is dead, all he gives you is a mass of uneatable meat and two huge and very heavy tusks that you will certainly never get home to England. Should you not obey the rules, you will surely die; either he will kneel you into pulp or swing you round by one foot, smashing you against a tree, screaming the while in a terrifying manner. The great hunter, Selous, and many others just once did not obey the rules they had made themselves and so ended their days.

Frank was wisely dead against following this elephant. He said an old lone bull could travel for days, but in the hope of his bringing us to water, he agreed reluctantly to go. We only took our two Dorobo trackers and two Swahilis, no Masai. The tracking was desperately slow for the ground was hard and dry. The Dorobos were of their best, we never lost the trail and towards evening saw him once. At mid-day next day he was still travelling and my water bottle was empty, though we still had a little in the gourd for the men with us. We decided the odds were against us and, to my great disappointment, turned back for home. Setting a good pace the Dorobos hurried us along; with nothing to look forward to, I soon began to suffer from thirst. Frank then ate some very sour apples, which nearly finished him. I had never been really thirsty before and did not enjoy it. At one moment I very nearly abandoned my rifle. As it got dark, using the stars and their instinct, the Dorobos slogged on. About midnight we saw our camp fire. I was completely exhausted and Frank could only totter along. Thus ended my one and only effort to shoot a lone elephant bull.

Fortunately the little water-hole had filled up, the boys having consumed all the salty urine. We rested for a couple of days and then carried on hacking out this useless track. You cannot hope to trek through the African bush for days with a lot of natives without losing a few. One trod on a sleeping mamba which promptly bit him; he was dead in a very short time. Another, carrying the raw leg of the eland, sat down to eat some of it, whereupon a lioness jumped on top of him and removed the meat and his head. Another of them, chopping wood for the camp fire, carelessly sliced his foot off; he bled to death. So Frank was most anxious not to lose the lot through lack of water. Then we came across two Masai; obviously they had drunk recently, but trying to find out where was exactly like asking the village idiot where the post office was. One Masai said it was four suns away, the other never even grunted. Nevertheless at the end of another two days, and four dead from thirst, we came across a large water-hole, obviously frequented by a vast number of game. The moon was now full and as our camp fires died down, all the animals in the world hurried down to drink. I was fascinated by all this, especially when a large full-maned lion and two lionesses appeared. He roared and I had never heard a hungry lion's full roar. It started quite close and then resounded round and round, a most awe-inspiring noise.

Frank had now lost his nerve. We knew we could not be much more than forty miles from the Ruvu River, if we trekked due north, so we dropped everything and set off. We reached the river all right and set up our camp a mile or so away from the river on account of the myriads of mosquitoes.

The railway ran about twenty miles north of the river. I said that I must leave for I had nearly expended my two months leave. Without much enthusiasm, a very frail bridge was made for me over this river which was infested with crocodiles. The forced march to the river had proved most exhausting; it was nearer eighty miles than forty but we were very fortunate in finding the occasional water-hole, chiefly thanks to our two Dorobo trackers, who followed the game trails; even so we lost several Swahili from exhaustion. I began to collect my best heads together and to tie them into loads, most awkward they proved. I decided to take four Swahili to carry them and my bedding roll, plus two only of the Masai chiefs' sons, who seemed to know where I was going and why.

One morning a few days later, an old Masai appeared. He showed us the tracks of a large buffalo bull, which came down from the bush every evening, swam across the river and mated with the cows belonging to the old man's herd. He besought us to kill the bull. Curiously enough Frank was quite willing to do this. After a meal on my last evening he and I, the two Dorobo and two Masai, made a little camp near where the bull was wont to cross the river. We were eaten alive by mosquitoes. Frank and I crouched under a very smelly blanket; sleep was impossible. Neither of us talked at all. I think we had both become devoted, though very silent friends, over the weeks. No bull, of course, appeared.

At dawn we returned to our camp. I collected my kit, my small party, crossed the bridge with the utmost care and set out for the railway line. I asked Frank what he intended to do and he said he was pondering over it but he thought he would send the Swahili over the river then move south himself until he finally reached home at Kibaya. I never saw him again.

The following is the account of Frank's death that afternoon, pieced together by Swinerton, the government tsetse fly officer, several days after it occurred. Margaret, Frank's sister, sent it to me in India six months later. It appears that after I had left, Frank collected the two Dorobos and his six chiefs' sons and, taking his rifle, set off to see if he could find the buffalo bull. The bush was very open and the tracking good. No man can tell why he did this. It was completely unlike him for he had never shot a beast of any sort all the time we had been together. They must have come up with the bull and Frank wounded him but not mortally. They then rested the customary three hours from noon to three o'clock to allow the wind to settle. The buffalo in the meantime had moved round noiselessly and was in fact not six feet from Frank, standing behind a thick bush. This is a common trait of wounded buffalo.

The Grave of Frank Spurrell, Kibaya

As Frank got up the bull charged, goring him mortally, and a battle to the death followed. The result was inevitable and ended in the death of the two valiant little Dorobo, four of the Masai chiefs' sons and finally of the bull himself. The news of this disaster reached Swinerton a hundred miles away by that completely unexplainable bush telegraph. When Swinerton arrived at the scene, there were only a few bones, Frank's rifle and the massive head of the buffalo to be found. Frank's grave today is at his old headquarters of Kibaya, marked by a large headstone sent out by his mother from Norfolk.

As my small party and I trekked along northwards towards the railway line, we came across some magnificent heads. I shot a good bush buck, an excellent Grant's gazelle and a fine impala, very much better heads than I had come across before, due probably to the fact that there were no lion between the river and the railway.

Reaching the railway line we set off to the south towards the port of Tanga. As we were considering camping for the night we came up with a maintenance gang. They had a bogey and were only too delighted to exchange it for the carcass of the bush buck. I bade my two Masai farewell, they turned and left me immediately. The Swahili were enchanted with the bogey and worked it madly for they were on their way home.

The following day we reached Hedaru much to the amazement and obvious annoyance of the little Indian stationmaster who hoped that he had seen the last of me. I sent a telegram to the schoolmaster, telling him to expect me on the next train and sat down to wait. The Swahilis disappeared, one of them presenting me with a long heavy stick bound round with grass, which he said my Dorobo had entrusted to his care for me. To my amazement when I had unwrapped it, I found that it was a nine foot Masai spear. I very much fear he must have killed one of my four chiefs' sons. However, I was delighted and it is still on the wall above my bed.

At last the train arrived and I was on my way south to the port of Tanga. I gazed at the passing bush country and thought of Reels, that white hunter, who had warned me of the constant danger from the dozing rhino. How right he had been. I never saw one broadside on, only its huge bottom and beastly little tail, as it hurtled along its horrid little path, leaving us pinned most painfully into thorn bushes.

Chapter 7

RETURNING TO INDIA

My friend the schoolmaster met me in Tanga with a truck, camp-kit, a cook and servant. He drove me down to the sea-shore, lovely sand and fluttering palm trees – almost unbelievable to me after the tough up-country bush land. For four days, we lazed, drank our fill from coconuts and hunted around for the beautiful sable antelope. I could have shot one but he was magnificent and the setting alongside the deep blue sea so wonderful that I had not the heart to kill him. I had killed enough lovely creatures.

My friend told me that a month earlier my ship, the Karoa had sprung a leak and had conveniently gone to the bottom of the sea, not far from Tanga port. He left me at a clean and spartan little hotel. He had been a true friend. I sent the regiment in India a wire, saying I was on my way back. I then called on the bank, which was prominent up and down the coast. There I found the most pleasant young men you could wish to find. Four of them, all from Cambridge, took charge of me. We found an Arab dhow setting sail for Zanzibar, so we boarded her. The locals on board were very smelly but pleasant. I thoroughly enjoyed the trip. In a good wind, those dhows fly along. I was most anxious to purchase a slave in Zanzibar; I have no idea why. But by the time we got there, it was evening and the slave market was empty, which was perhaps very fortunate. The town was fascinating with plenty of large white-washed houses, semi-fortified with huge ancient doors. Crowds of pretty dangerous looking people were everywhere.

We met a very ancient European of sorts. He said he had been there since the days of Queen Victoria and he probably had. He invited us to his huge house, gave us a very good meal, washed down with an excellent strong brew, so we spent the night on one of his many verandahs, overlooking the sea. Next morning we had a wonderful very fast sail back to Tanga. It was my last night so my companions feasted me far too generously. At a very late hour we penetrated a most unsavoury house of no doubt very ill repute. There was a mass of very silent evil looking men, each with a long curved knife in his belt. Then on to a small stage came the largest, blackest negress imaginable. Completely naked, she turned her back on the audience and solemnly rotated her right buttock to the right and her left buttock to the left. This amused me very much; she kept time with the drums going faster and faster. I cheered madly and had to be dragged out by the others, for the locals were definitely not amused. Finally they put me to bed still singing 'Rule Britannia'.

Next morning quite early my companions came to take me to a small steamer on its way to Mombasa. I bade them go away and leave me to die in peace. I could not stand, I felt and hoped for an early death. My head, I believed, was cloven with an axe. They went away and so did the steamer. Some days later, I managed to reach the small hospital where I met a very large bearded man, lying in a very small bed. He told me that a rhino had holed him in the thigh and, if I wished, he would be happy to take me north to Mombasa in a dhow which he had purchased in order to get to a larger hospital as soon as possible. He told me that one morning when inspecting his sisal, a large rhino emerged behind him and just came straight for him. In spite of his being a varsity running blue, the rhino got him, making a large round hole in his thigh. I thought him a most jovial human being and I thoroughly enjoyed the trip.

There were no steamers from Mombasa to India for a couple of months or so. However, there was a small coaster leaving for the Seychelle Islands very shortly. On this I embarked, as, although I had no idea where the islands were, I was sure they must be nearer India than where I was now. Sleeping on the deck with a mass of Indians and a large crate containing my half-cured antelope heads was not very pleasant. However, all bad things end and one morning we reached a really lovely island, lots of palms, flowers and silver sand. An immaculate little Frenchman in spotless white drill came aboard. He approached me, asking me what on earth was I doing in the Seychelles. I told him I wished to return to my regiment in India. 'Well,' he said, 'there is a boat of sorts due to leave for Bombay in three weeks time; in the meantime you had better come and stay with me.' My Frenchman flatly refused to have my case of horns anywhere near him, for they smelt abominably, so we left it in a go-down. He had a very smart dog-cart with a young man dressed in white, and a groom who ran alongside.

His bungalow was charming with a deep verandah and I got a glimpse of a lovely garden stretching down to the shore. He offered me a shower before breakfast, giving me some beautiful silk-initialled underclothes, straight from the Rue St Honoré, and a beach coat. I am sure I smelt almost as bad as my horns. His name was Christophe; he had landed there for ten minutes and stayed ten years. Just as I was enjoying beautiful hot coffee, in walked the most ravishing girl I had seen in my life. She was Mara, a Creole; she was beautiful, small dark, huge eyes and skin like satin, wearing a long white silk dress, the top half so low that her charming breasts were totally exposed. She was very happy and immensely amused by me. I suppose I was pretty solemn. I could not take my eyes off her, or attempt to eat any more delicious breakfast. In fact every moment of my stay with them, I lived in a delightful deeply scented daze. They were both charming to me; every time Christophe saw me he burst out laughing.

He said that he simply could not imagine how anyone in the world, much less a prosaic English officer, could have been so stupid as to have gone through all the hardship I had. To what end?

They took me out at all sorts of times to meals with other Frenchmen who seemed to have stayed on after their jobs had finished, maybe some years ago. There must have been a lot of natives living there too, but I saw no town, maybe a few small villages. The weather was warm and sunny and then a good shower of rain every day. My host warned me not to bathe in the tempting blue sea, on account of sharks, land crabs and other deadly things. What did I care, I had never been so well looked after.

A little Indian came in and made some white duck suits for me and I am sure Mara burnt all my bush kit for I never saw it again. Every evening when we finally went to bed, Mara came and wished me good-night and kissed me sweetly. She treated me exactly as if I were her fourteen-year old son, but I wasn't; I was much older and in a state of near delirium. When I tried to explain this to her, she merely laughed and flowed away. Christophe did nothing and wanted for nothing. I really don't believe he ever realised the wonder of the island on which he lived, the sheer beauty of the countless gaily coloured birds, the happy natives almost as gaily arrayed, but the time came when I had to leave.

My last day arrived. I knew that I had to go, though both Christophe and Mara beseeched me to stay for at least a year. The journey home was completely uneventful, then one evening I walked into the mess at Kirkee. I found my battery had left Secunderabad, which was very sad. I think the only two people who were glad to see me were my bearer and maybe the colonel.

The tempo of my daily life very quickly returned to normal. I even tried to learn some gunnery. Then one morning I found a little old man sitting on the steps of my bungalow. I remembered him months ago at Secunderabad when he had told me that he wished to give me a present, but that he would have to go a long, long way for it. I gave him 15 rupees and I never thought I should see him again. He solemnly produced a bundle of rags and out of it a ceremonial elephant bell of hand beaten brass, certainly stolen out of one of the native princes' elephant stables. It must have been made at least two hundred years ago. I was delighted and presented him with 30 rupees for he must have travelled several hundred miles.

This was all now a completely different life. I no longer wanted to shoot gazelle. The teak jungles of the Western Ghats certainly held bison and no doubt tiger, but for me they were unobtainable so I made do with snipe and duck where I could find them. I took up tent-pegging with our Indian drivers every Thursday morning and became reasonably proficient at it. I had an excellent charger which rode dead straight.

The 3rd Cavalry was the Indian cavalry regiment in the Poona garrison. All the sowars were recruited from Trans-Indus and it seemed to me to consist almost entirely of Pathans. I took my troop of guns out with them on exercises. I had also made great friends with the sister of one of the squadron commanders, who was visiting the regiment. I liked them all although I never really felt at home with their sowars. All Pathans have one maddening habit: when they have nothing to do, they sit round a fire and chant. The chant is always the same, accompanied by a one-stringed instrument rather like a frying pan. The chant is of course in Pushtu and when translated goes – 'There is a boy across the river, with a bottom like a peach, but alas I cannot swim.'

When the 3rd Cavalry Regiment held their regimental mounted sports, they opened certain events, like show jumping, tent-pegging etc., to the whole garrison. I went in for the tent-pegging and finished in the last four. It was won by the regimental subhadar major, a huge man with immense whiskers. We were to meet again.

I was told off the record that a signal had come through from army headquarters saying that if Lieutenant Daniell applied to join the relief column of the Chitral Garrison, it would be granted. The column marched through the Hindu Kush, taking three months or more. It passed through the wildest region in the world. Ibex, ovia, ammon and Marco Polo sheep, with their immense horns, abounded. I tackled my major at once, who agreed that he had received such a message but he had replied that I was not available. To miss such a wonderful trip was too much, but he was adamant and in my opinion a very stupid senior officer.

Christmas 1926 approached and I seemed to have quite a lot of cash in the bank, so I purchased a very small Fiat car. Unwisely I asked my co-subaltern Sinclair to drive down with me to Goa; charming fellow as he was, he had no real interest in stalking bison or any other large beast.

The teak forests down the Western Ghats were marvellous, enormous trees, and underneath them, bamboo forests, with wild elephants abounding. If there were any jungle tribes, they remained out of sight. I sent the word round for a local shikari but no one came. We stayed for a few days in a forest rest house, perched on a little knoll overlooking a fair sized pool, where three streams met, a most restful and lovely spot, completely wasted on me. At least every day on my way home about mid-day, I stripped and swam across the pool. There were no crocodiles or other pests. Sinclair strayed off into Goa, visiting the local headman and came back bedecked with huge garlands. A very stupid man of no account turned up, and appeared to think we wanted to shoot some of the wild elephants, which of course, we were not allowed to do. There was a herd of about fifty nearby and he took us to have a look at them. We carefully kept upwind of them, the going under the bamboo was completely noiseless. Anyway they appeared harmless, much taken up with a little baby elephant who would not go into a pool and have a bathe unless severely prodded from behind.

They were very different from the African wild elephants.

I saw no game; we were eaten alive by mosquitoes by day and by night so we drove back to Bangalore, stopping on the way at a swampy jeel where we shot a hundred snipe and, with our last 12-bore cartridge, a large cobra. The trip anyway convinced me that those teak forests were no good to me. We gave all the snipe to a couple of very pleasant gunner officers' wives, who gave us an excellent dinner in exchange.

We got back in time for the men's Christmas dinner and the new year birthday parade, which was very hot and very tiring, starting at 5 a.m. I was still mad at not being allowed to go to Chitral.

Polo started, Government House opened up and Lord and Lady Lloyd arrived from Bombay. Lord Lloyd wanted a No. 1 for his polo team and Lady Lloyd wanted an amenable ADC. I was told to report to Government House where I met Colonel Previte, a marine; curiously we met again years later in the Sovereign's Bodyguard and became great friends. In no time I was fitted out in the immaculate white uniform of an ADC, gold lines, sword and huge topee with its gold spike.

My duties were not arduous, though Lady Lloyd was very strict. She clamped down in no mean way on any budding friendships her ADCs might have in view. We won several polo tournaments; life at Government House was very comfortable and the food excellent, so I very much enjoyed my six months tour. I was thankful not to have to return with them to Bombay where it was so hot and humid.

Before they left, we had to organise the Poona Horse Show, the largest of its kind in Southern India. It attracted a very large number of entries and for us a great deal of hard work. Several of my friends of the Saugor days arrived and one of them told me that Rex Peel won the Hunter Class with my horse Vision at the Delhi Horse Show and that it had been purchased for the viceroy. Good for Rex!

I entered for the tent-pegging, a very popular event. After dozens of heats, the subhadar-major of the 3rd Cavalry and I were left in the final. The whole regiment was there in the evening to cheer on their subhadar. I saw nearby my orderly and our Indian officer, madly excited, holding my spear. The subhadar-major and I went through the whole gamut again: three tent-pegs, three half pegs, three quarter pegs and lastly three laths. I was lucky and won by a lath. The old man was a good loser; he came and congratulated me, with tears in his eyes, as he got the umbrella with a gold band and I got a very nice gold pencil with Lord Lloyd's initials. I still have it.

The captain of my battery was a quiet, pleasant intelligent officer. He was only interested in promotion to high rank. He passed easily into the staff college and for many years passed out of my life. We met again in the western desert during the 1939-45 war. General Montgomery wished to make a diversion in the north of the Mareth Line, along the Wadi Zessor. It was to be a three-battalion attack to commence as the guns opened fire. My old captain was in charge of the guns. At the last moment, General Montgomery observed that the Germans had produced three times as many tanks as he had anticipated. He certainly could not afford the loss of his three precious battalions so he ordered an immediate cancellation of the attack. The orders reached two battalions and two thirds of the guns and were obeyed. They did not reach the third battalion and its supporting guns. Peter Gregson and I had wandered up the Wadi Zessor to watch the attack. This was most unwise as a great many of our shells fell short into the wadi, followed by a fusillade from the German 88mms. Monty arrived in a very bad humour; he managed to get the advancing battalion to withdraw and so avoid its total destruction. He then sacked my old captain in no mean terms. We thought we would be safer out of the way. Nothing could have been truer, so we emulated the dead lying about in the bushes. I was very sorry for Brigadier Hall.

Captain Francis Foljambe MC arrived in due course, tall, very good-looking, excelling in all ball games; he was much liked by all the battery. He brought his pleasant wife with him. Alas he only stayed a few months, for when he applied for leave to join his brother on a big game shoot in East Africa, the battery commander turned it down, saying that he had not been with the battery long enough to justify two months leave. Captain Foljambe responded by retiring from the army altogether and going off to East Africa. The Royal Regiment lost a first class, highly intelligent officer. His wife asked me to go and see her mother and sister when I returned to England which I did and thoroughly enjoyed their company.

The whole regiment moved north to Jhansi, a very hot station, which had not changed at all from the days before the Mutiny. The small city of Jhansi was famous for its magnificent fort and for the princess who had defended it most gallantly and most unwisely on behalf of the mutinous Peshwah at the outbreak of the Mutiny.

The small game shooting was excellent. My cousin and I shot nineteen different varieties of game birds in one day. I knew that I would be returning to England later on in the spring and that I must have one more try at a tiger. There were plenty of forest blocks to be had nearby so I applied for the nearest, sending there an old and skilled shikari to spy out the land. After a couple of weeks, he reported back that he had found no trace of tiger but there were a few bison, which I had never shot, bear and sembhar. One day as I was resting in a glade, a fine lone old bison bull walked across towards me. I took plenty of time and caution, fired and killed him stone dead.

The forest block had a large river, now mostly dry, running along one side. This was in fact a deterrent as it made it very difficult to locate the game I wanted. At last we came across the pug-marks of a tigress; from then on I never fired another shot. I wanted to keep the forest absolutely quiet. She proved most difficult, there one week and gone the next but she always returned. I put out some 'kills' for her which she never touched and I never found a single carcass of any of the deer which she had killed. The forest was mostly of sal, deciduous trees with hard wood like teak from which all the leaves were falling, so there was practically no shade. My excellent shikari said that he was sure that the tigress spent the hottest part of the day lying in a pile of rocks. To approach these rocks noiselessly was impossible on account of the sal leaves which exploded like a rifle-shot, as you trod on them.

I determined to sweep two paths up to the rocks one evening, clear of every leaf and then stalk the tigress at mid-day next day. I explained this to my cousin who flatly refused to have anything to do with it. He said that it was asking for trouble, in spite of my telling him that on no account would I risk a shot that was not fatal. All went to plan, my shikari was certain the tigress was there but we just could not make her out. The stripes on her body were a perfect blending with the dappled shade. After a couple of hours of intense exasperation, we moved noiselessly away.

Now my wonderful time in India was drawing to a close and sadly I had to go home to England. Never has a young man had such a marvellous time as I had in India for the few years that I was there.

Chapter 8

BACK IN ENGLAND

I arrived home in England at the beginning of June 1928 and went straight up to Anglesey where I found all my family at Pencraig, very well. It is a lovely time of year in Anglesey and my mother and I went down to the cliffs. All the sea birds were nesting among the sea pinks. It was extremely difficult not to tread on some of the nests.

I was posted to Woolwich and when I got there I couldn't have disliked it more. I had a horrid little room with just the bare essentials; after my lovely bungalow at Kirkee, I found it very hard to bear. There was a pair of cobra who sat daily on the cool stones by the steps of my bungalow. I never saw them together so I did not dare shoot one as its mate would wander everywhere looking for it. They did not make me love cobra any more. There was a tree in the garden, from which which hundreds of fruit bats hung upside down all day long, looking too terrible for words but now I missed it. I yearned to be back in India but I knew I must be in England if I was to get my 'jacket'.

The Woolwich Mess was certainly the best to be found in England, with fine dining tables and three fabulous chandeliers, presented by royalty who frequently dined there a century before. Royalty also presented very colourful crimson and yellow livery for the mess servants. Woolwich itself was a poor place; there was nowhere to ride and nothing much to do and the job that I was given couldn't have been more boring. I had at least a dozen squads of young recruits who were there for fourteen weeks to learn marching, rifle drill and how to clean their boots. None of these things had I any interest in at all. In the Woolwich Mess about a hundred people came in to lunch and only six or so for dinner and they were the ones who had spent all their money. The total cost of our excellent meals in the mess was a shilling per day.

I found a dozen or so subalterns of my own age. Dudley Clarke was a most gifted and charming man. Long afterwards he became Winston Churchill's right hand man during the 1939 war. Another one was Holmes Watson who was senior to me and had been posted to India for the first time. He had eluded it up to now. He drank like a fish and thought he had better take his coffin with him. A coffin was being made by the carpenters in the mess and we visited it periodically, twenty of us, to see if it fitted Holmes Watson, who was rather plump; having drunk an enormous amount of beer with the carpenters, it always seemed too small for him. Another most delightful man, Harry Gummer, had lost an eye in some episode which he was reticent about. He was very good looking and great company. He wasn't what you would call a very ardent soldier but he could charm the birds off any tree. Lord Beaverbrook took him on as a social secretary for a short time and asked him one day to look after his latest girl-friend for the week-end, as he had to go abroad on business. Harry, of course, took the girl to Deauville where he met Lord Beaverbrook with an even newer girl-friend, in the passage on their way back from their bath. Needless to say, he was asked to leave on Lord Beaverbrook's return to London. There was another delightful man, whose name I have forgotten, but he took one of the Pearson girls out to a supper one night in the country and, on the way back, he ran into a donkey cart, killing the donkey and thoroughly upsetting its very old owner. As he wasn't insured and Miss Pearson was considerably shocked, it was a very expensive evening for him. So much so that he decided to leave the regiment and find some other pastime. He went to Canada where he couldn't even find a job sweeping the streets. However he drifted across to Beverley Hills where he married a film actress. After a very short time they divorced and he married a much more famous film actress and the two of them were extremely well off living there happily ever after.

I yearned to be back in India. I was terribly bored with training these recruits. I never knew their names and they all looked alike to me so I had a look round for something a bit more amusing and I found that in a very short time I had a lot of friends in London and I became a name on a list for dances and dinners. I went to London every evening and came back to Woolwich about 6.30 in the morning. I enjoyed myself very much; it was only for a short time, just for the two months of the season but I did meet a lot of friends and a number of people who became great friends afterwards.

As the autumn came, I bought a couple of hunters and an old Chrysler car and I decided to hunt in Essex, keeping my horses at the Green Man at Harlow. The master of the Essex Hunt and many others were very kind to me and asked me to shoot very frequently before we hunted. Far too much ploughed land for my liking but it was the nearest hunt to Woolwich. I began to look seriously for a steeplechaser because I realised now was the time to make my name known but I had great difficulty in finding one that I could afford. With the help of Mark Ruddock, I found a horse called Glasshealey, good looking, good jumper, fast – but an idiot of a horse! Unless he was in front he used to look at the other horses when he came to a fence and invariably went down!

I rode in many races that autumn and the early spring and had a large number of falls. Mark Ruddock had two good horses and when he smashed his collar bone, he asked me to ride them for him. I should have won the Gunner Gold Cup on one of them, had I been a little more experienced on the Sandown Course.

I renewed my acquaintance with Nell Faljombe's sister, Betty Priestman and visited her home and parents in Co. Durham. Her uncle owned a private pack of fox-hounds, the Grays of Derwent and her brother hunted them. Everyone knew everyone else and the country was stiff, mostly very high stone walls and timber. They were exceedingly nice to me, an intruder into their land. Betty was surrounded with a lot of very ardent and extremely nice young men and they were skilled over those big stone walls but not so skilled over timber, so in order to hold my end up, I used to take the gates and let them take the walls. This wasn't appreciated by all of them. I stayed with them for Christmas and then Betty and I got engaged. I took her to Anglesey after Christmas to meet my family who were charmed by her but the weather was appalling. It never stopped raining for one moment; however, that really didn't make any difference to us. We were to be married in the spring and we both started looking forward to it. Betty and I went to hunt balls all over the place, up in the north and elsewhere. I bought a very expensive and resplendent pink coat which she said was essential; I was very proud to wear it. I was fortunate to win the Members' Race, the Brays of Derwent Point-to-Point on Douglas Nicholson's horse. My own horse, Glasshealey was no better than he was before. He gave me some more crashing falls, breaking a collar bone and two ribs. Then came the Gunner Meeting and Betty came down to Sandown. I had several rides but was unsuccessful, chiefly I think because I was so bound up with plaster that I could hardly ride at all.

Betty and I had a great wedding in April, on a fine cold Northumberland day, masses of presents and the hunt's servants blew us away. Betty's father had given her a new car and we drove down to York where we spent our first night and very pleasant it all was but we were very, very tired. We had a lovely honeymoon in Italy and couldn't have enjoyed it more. While we were away, Betty's kind mother furnished a little house for us, near Woolwich so that when we came back the house was all ready, with servants there, and we just walked straight in. Fortunately there were some stables at the bottom of the garden so I could keep a couple of horses there and my groom. Betty and I used to ride out in the mornings before breakfast and jump the jumps that were in the fields around the farm.

Our first summer of married life passed very pleasantly. I got rid of Glasshealey and, in spite of help from several quarters, I failed to find anything that I could afford to take his place. In the early autumn I got my 'jacket', which I had set my heart on ever since I had become a gunner officer. I was posted to 'D' Battery Royal Horse Artillery and I was overjoyed. The next five years in 'D' Battery could not have been happier for us both. We rented a nice Georgian house in Farnham with a lovely garden, as the 3rd Regiment Royal Horse Artillery were stationed at Aldershot. The Horse Artillery is the corps d'élite of the Royal Regiment, officers and NCOs hand picked, with the gunners of a very high quality. The batteries, or troops as they were originally named, formed the integral unit, rather than the regiment. The morale of each battery with its long history behind it was very high; one moved at the double, one's turnout was impeccable and everything one thought or did was to the best of one's ability for the enhancement of the battery.

It was exceedingly hard work. There were no two ways about it. You were in charge of every parade and had to stand on your own feet and train your own men and horses. This was all very different from what I had experienced before. In a very short time you were expected to know everything about the men in your section, to command, by example, their loyalty and confidence, equally if not more so, the peculiarities of every horse under your command. For on the stamina and fitness of each horse depended the guns, 13-pounders; they were most beautifully kept.

The other two batteries in the 3rd Regiment RHA were 'M' Battery and 'J' Battery. They were still there when I commanded the regiment several years later in the western desert campaign. All the officers in the regiment were extremely efficient and delightful to know. Bob Manseugh was senior subaltern of 'D' Battery. Years afterwards he became the master gunner at St James Park and his efficiency and pleasant manner had not changed.

My battery commander was Tom Sebag-Montefiore with an MC and DSO of the 1914 war, won at a very early age. 'D' Battery was his life, he served it well; he never forgave a mistake and only tolerated the best: not an easy taskmaster. For fifteen years, Charles Allfrey was Captain of 'D' Battery, without exception the kindest, most efficient and charming man I have ever met. He became a corps commander before the end of the 1939 war. He married the sister of Jack Scudamore, my bosom companion at St Aubyn's.

In the early summer, riding down Salisbury Plain, as we passed the race course of Tweeseldown, Sebag rode up to me and said, 'Bob, I expect you to win a race here next spring for 'D' Battery.'

I replied, 'If I can only find a horse, sir, I will do that.' I found the horse and won the big race in the spring, the Open Services Cup. I repeated this the following year with another horse, Riposte, also winning several other races. Sebag was delighted. On our march down to Salisbury Plain, we stopped at a small stream to water the horses, Betty arrived there with coffee and rolls for all the officers, which was most appreciated, in spite of the dogs who, in their excitement, nearly stampeded the horses, much to the annoyance of Battery Sergeant-Major Cox, who was certainly a demi-god.

On our return from practice camp, Sebag insisted on us procuring some polo ponies. With a cavalry brigade at Aldershot, polo was flourishing and he wanted at least two of 'D' Battery's subalterns playing in the subalterns regimental. He got me as I knew the game but he wasn't really satisfied, especially as we failed to win the tournament at Ranelagh.

Leave in 'D' Battery, Sebag explained to me, was only given to officers who went hunting and when he asked what I was going to do, 'Go hunting,' I said.

So Squealer Wheeler and I set off to the Grafton country to find a small hunting lodge to rent for a month. As we passed a rather nice looking woman, wearing fabulous pearls, who was collecting firewood in the ditch, we stopped to ask her the way. 'Why on earth do you want to go there?' she asked. When we told her, she snorted and told us we would do far better by taking her house. We viewed it and took it for a month at £5 per week. She went off to her husband in Ceylon, leaving the key under the mat. The cottage had really priceless furniture in it, not very well cared for. Towards the end of November, we rode the horses, some ten of them, up there, eighty miles on a hard road, and Betty and I settled in.

Lord Hillingdon, the Master of the Grafton Hunt, liked to have a few individualistic soldiers in his field who always rode their own line across country, thus saving his fences, for the field was always about a hundred. Betty and I thoroughly enjoyed our first season. She had her own horse, which I found pulled like a train but fortunately was an excellent jumper for the Grafton country held big fences and very stiff timber. Every weekend, two or three subalterns would drive up from Aldershot, hunt their horses and stay the weekend with us. The RHA grooms loved it all. They made friends with all the local girls, no doubt shooting a big line about their horses and their officers; best of all no sergeant-major to harry them. They took whatever accommodation was available, sometimes a harness room, more often the loft above the stables.

In all the years we were there, I never had a single complaint from any of them. We did this every winter we were at Aldershot, making many friends who lived in the Grafton country. Invariably they invited us to lunch on a Sunday, always followed by the ritual of visiting their stables. Bobbie Pennington, who lived quite near, with a delightful small family, was second in the National on his hunter Bovril II and, had he been really fit, I think he would have won it. We always hacked out to the meets, sometimes fourteen miles and hacked home again, so that the grooms were fresh when the horses came in. There were no horse boxes in those days, though there was one old gentleman who had a covert-hack, probably the last in England, on which he cantered to the meets, having invariably consumed a breakfast of mutton chops or beef steak, washed down with a complete bottle of claret. He was rising eighty years old.

One year when we were housed in Lady Furneaux's delightful little house in Brackley, there was a very hard and enduring frost. I immediately drove off to shoot duck and geese on the North Norfolk coast. Tom Sebag rang up to know why I had not returned to Aldershot, did I not know that leave was only given to his officers to hunt. I was to return immediately. When Betty told him that that was impossible because she did not know where I was, he nearly had apoplexy. In the meanwhile, I had made my way to Blakeney, a very small village. Every evening and every morning, one of the Long brothers, all wildfowlers, took me out with them over the marshes.

One night of full moon, when the harbour was frozen over, we shot wigeon until 1 a.m. and picked up fifty-four. Sam Long asked me if I would like to go punt gunning with him in his punt and try the estuary, where the duck were sitting in huge packs. On our way he told me how and when to fire the enormous gun. I was certainly scared of it. I knew it had remained loaded at least ten days and I was most apprehensive as to which end all the shot would come out. The cold was intense and if it had not been for his labrador who lay on top of me, I should have called the whole thing off.

We wormed our way quite close to a pack of wigeon, which blackened the sea. At last as they rose, I pulled the trigger. Wigeon fell everywhere, the labrador jumped overboard, taking the gun with her. It certainly was exciting. As the punt sank, Sam said not to worry as we were on a sand bank and, unless the wind got up, we would be able to walk ashore in a couple of hours. Sam no doubt was used to standing up to his waist in the icy sea in the middle of winter. I was not and vowed never again to do this. Should I have the luck to get back to the Black Bull, run by his nice sister, I decided I would doss down in front of the roaring stove and stay there for the next two days, with a bottle of whisky and a bottle of rum.

With the car full of duck and geese, I drove back to London, where Betty was staying with her mother. I presented her mother with a very large pinkfooted goose, which she did not want at all, and on we drove to Farnham. Tom Sebag had gone off to Monte Carlo, for he was a great gambler, so all was well.

During the next year our life passed very pleasantly. We worked very hard. Betty entertained as often as she could in our charming old house. Ascot came; I drove the coach every day from Windsor, a lovely drive through the park to a special enclosure opposite the winning post, reserved for members of the Coaching Club; then a fast drive home, change into full dress for the Torchlight Tattoo. This was an extremely effective sight for the public. The guns were lit up but the manoeuvring at full gallop in the pitch dark, especially the scissors, was dangerous beyond words. Someone always invited us on to a very late supper, so we were lucky to get a few hours sleep.

At the back of my mind was my urgent need to find a horse on which to win the Royal Artillery Gold Cup at Sandown in the spring. This was the last of the three things I had set out to accomplish. Peter Payne-Galleway, an excellent G.R. in the 11th Hussars, wrote to me saying, if I was interested, he intended to part with Backsight, on whom he had won many point-to-points though he doubted that Backsight would ever win a steeplechase at his present age of thirteen. I went down to see Peter and the horse, which was just what I needed.

I had no further ambition, except the Gunner Gold Cup, so I bought Backsight, never imagining for one moment what a good horse he could have been when young or what a sensation he was to make. I hunted him that season with the Grafton. I did know that his near fore tendon had put him out of action at least once, so I ought to have been a great deal more careful of him than I was. Sure enough on our last day's hunting, we had a fast nine mile point from

Weedon Bushes; only four of the field finished, including Lord Hillingdon. The next morning, Backsight was lame. I knew at once it was that tendon. I asked Male, the best veterinary officer I have ever met, to come over. His verdict, to fire and blister the leg and put him away for a year, was what I had expected. I told him that this was quite impossible as I needed the horse to run at Sandown in March. 'Personally,' he said, 'I do not think that is possible. However, I will do my best and I will only blister the tendon, then we will wait and see.' I had met Eric Steadal, whom I liked immensely. He had a few horses in training at Lewes in Sussex. I told him the story and asked him if he would train Backsight later on in the spring.

Fortunately the fates were on our side. He was so successful that I ran him at Tweeseldown and won the Open Services Cup for 'D' Battery in early March. Eric then came to me and said he wanted me to run Backsight in the Grand Military Gold Cup. I was dead against this, as it was two weeks before the one I so badly wanted to win. Further I knew I could not make the weight. An unknown hunter was awarded a very low weight in this valuable race. In the end Eric persuaded me to let him run and to ask Peter Payne-Galleway, a very light weight, to ride him. I stipulated that whatever the result, Backsight must be allowed to run his own race and must not be pressed. Peter agreed.

Friday, 17th March came, a pouring wet day, very heavy going, a very big field for the Gold Cup, including a horse ridden by Roscoe Harvey just home from India. Peter kept Backsight right at the back and out of trouble, for a lot of horses came down, then he let him go and he won the Grand Military Gold Cup for me. It was sensational, no Gunner had owned the winner of this race for many years, and no subaltern had ever won it. Peter had ridden a very well judged race, he knew his old horse so well. Of course, I was delighted; so was Sebag who insisted on my giving the whole of 'D' Battery a dinner with limitless ale.

At the back of my mind I was apprehensive, for a fortnight later as I rode down to the start, I knew that he was a hot favourite. The fates were against us; I was out in front when he made a bad mistake at a plain bush fence and down I came. I vaulted up again but could only make third with no stirrups. I took a long time to get over this disappointment.

I rode Backsight in one last race, the Tarporley Hunt Cup, on a rough course near Chester. My sister Clare and my young brother, Tony, whom I really did not know at all, drove over from Anglesey to see me win! There was a good young steeplechaser called Quick Sand, ridden by a professional jockey, named Blissill in the race. I am certain that Quick Sand had never been seen in any hunting field in his life. He was a fast but very erratic jumper, I gave him too much rope and he beat me by a neck. Most disappointing for both of us. I sold Backsight to Lord Penrhyn. Sadly he never ran again.

Out of the blue, a woman in Dorset wrote to me saying she had a grey thoroughbred pony, five years old, which would make me an excellent polo pony. How right she was. Fireman became the best polo pony I ever had. He loved the game, was wise and fast, always following the ball himself. Unfortunately in spite of all our efforts, we only managed to be beaten again by one of the cavalry regiments in the final of the Subalterns' Inter-Regimental at Ranelagh. Tony Sebag was very disappointed and so was I.

Early in the spring of 1934, the secretary of the Hexham Race Course, where I had taken a crashing fall on Glasshealey some time before, rang me up. He told me that Jack Fawcus had a most promising young jumper five years old, and urged me to go and have a ride on him. This I did next day, travelling all night. I made my way to the Fawcus homestead, which proved to be a large farm, romantically situated right down on the sea in Northumberland. On my arrival, I found the horses already saddled up. Young Fawcus and I set off. They had trimmed the large natural fences for two and a half miles. Fawcus set a good strong gallop and I would much like to have had some breakfast as the fences were daunting.

Riposte jumped like a stag and I loved him, a good bay, short-backed with strong hindquarters, about the same size as Backsight. I purchased him while unsaddling and then ate a huge breakfast. He was to become one of the best hunter-chasers in the land that year. He won every race I rode him in, he was second in the Grand Military Gold Cup and very nearly won it. A fortnight later on a lovely spring day at Sandown Park, I rode Riposte down to the start for the Gunner Gold Cup. Nineteen runners, a record entry, and this time I rode a sensible race. I did not let Riposte go into the lead until the last fence and went on to win comfortably. At last I was satisfied.

During the early summer I did not really know what to do with Riposte. He didn't at all like being my parade charger, the thunder of the gun teams behind him at the gallop unnerved him and he was apt to go off like a rocket, just anywhere. In the autumn I would be promoted to captain and would have to leave 'D' Battery for a year or so. I had no idea where I might be going, so very foolishly when Peter Cazalet and Mildmay offered me a big sum for him, I let him go. He was certainly the best horse I ever owned, a beautiful jumper over fences, but a most difficult horse to hunt, except perhaps in country like the Cottesmore. Perhaps the real reason was I had done enough of it for the time being, the many falls, the anxiety to win and that foolish race I rode on Backsight, which I could well do again, influenced me too much. These days at Aldershot were hectic, one thing followed another so quickly. I really hardly had time to think straight, but I was learning some essential gunnery.

One morning at stables, Tom Sebag was inspecting my horses. He turned to me and said, 'Where is number 48?'

I replied, 'I have no idea, sir. Perhaps he is being shod. I will go and see.' Now our sergeant farrier was excellent, though very short tempered, and one thing he could not stand was any of the subalterns asking him questions. He threw down his tools, a red-hot horse-shoe missed me by inches and he stormed out. Number 48 was certainly not there and I became slightly uneasy, especially when I found that Driver Hansome, his wheel-driver, had not been seen during the last thirty-six hours. Next morning there was a postcard for me from a small village near Taunton, it was from Driver Hansome saying he was so sorry, but his father was ill and, having no money he rode down there. Would I please come quickly, he had only three shillings to leave number 48 for his food, and that would not last him long. The only thing Sebag said was, 'It's your horse and driver, go and get them both back, Bob.'

Then one Monday morning, my young horse-holder, Driver Pritchard, and two of my signallers were missing. They were all three excellent young soldiers. I got through to the police at Wapping, where Pritchard lived and they went to see his parents. All they could gather was that all three had drunk a great deal of cider and gone off to look at the ships, down Wapping way. Not a word was heard of them for eight months, then the police rang up to say that my three soldiers were in the police station, begging to be arrested at all costs. It appeared that the boys had walked up the gangway of a large sailing ship, no-one was about, they lay down on some coils of rope and dropped asleep. The ship sailed quietly down the river. Treated as stowaways, they were at every sailor's beck and call, with only hard tack to eat. They were never allowed ashore and were very thankful to have reached land again. This was the best joke 'D' Battery had had for many years. Wherever they went they were met with calls of 'Up the rigging, sailor boys.'

At the end of the summer I was promoted to captain and posted as a territorial adjutant to the Westmoreland and Cumberland Yeomanry. Betty was delighted. She found a charming little house near Carlisle, where we were soon installed with our horses, my grey polo pony and our spaniels.

Our life had dramatically changed yet once again. The county was full of charming people who could not have been kinder or more welcoming to us, however mad on horses they thought us. The country was beautiful though rather wet at times. Most people's main joy was in their lovely gardens and excellent shoots. Our garden, though quite small, held nesting game of every sort, a pair of woodcock, curlew, plover, pheasants and partridges, yet our labrador never touched them. The many friends we made up there have remained with us to this day. I shot every day in the winter. My most memorable day was when Herchard Mousey Heysham took me out to shoot pinkfooted geese on his marsh in the Solway Firth. It was a fine sunny morning on my birthday, 15th October. Herchard said there were about three thousand geese on the marsh, yet not one was to be seen as we walked out for about a mile. He showed me a small rivulet to crouch down in and adjured me not to lose my head when the tide came in, flooding the marsh to about 3ft 6in. He suggested that four geese would be about as much as I could carry home.

Soon the tide started to flow in, lifting the geese off the sandbanks lower down the firth. For three hours in small batches they flew over my head, some settled around me. I was fascinated, they are such beautiful, enchanting birds. I shot my prescribed four and then just stood there and watched them while to my horror the whole marsh was covered with water. About three o'clock the tide turned, thank goodness, and soon I was able to 'slosh' over to join Herchard. We ate our lunch on part of an old boat, then started for home; certainly four geese were enough to carry, they weighed a ton. We dumped them on the sea wall, then returned to await the duck, mostly mallard as they flew in on the evening flight, hundreds of them in long lines. A few, enough to keep us busy, came down to drink on the pools where we were. As darkness fell, we collected all the birds we had shot and staggered back the two or three miles to Castletown. A true Scottish meal: tea strong, laced with whisky, awaited us. I telephoned to Betty. I was utterly exhausted so I stayed the night with Herchard.

At St Aubyn's I had made many friends, among them Boy and Joe. We three were inseparable. They both went on to Dartmouth and into the navy. Boy was outstandingly clever, though somewhat unamenable to discipline, while Joe, a red-haired Irishman, had a temper that had to be seen to be believed. Not unnaturally, the navy had had enough of them both by the end of war. The navy was Boy's entire life and he never got over it. Joe went happily back to Castle Shane where he fought the Sinn Fein, who promptly burnt his castle to the ground. Boy's father was a charming, brilliant man; his mother a concert pianist, very beautiful and very intolerant of other women, young and old. All his three brothers had brains far above the average, which I fancy was their downfall. Kia, the second son, somehow or other met Louise, a friend of my sister, a Canadian, most attractive, amusing – and very, very rich. After their engagement, Kia wired to Boy, who was in the USA, to return home at once to be his best man. Boy duly arrived, fell madly in love with Louise, completely mesmerising her, married her with Kia looking ghastly as best man, and their very wistful father who, I have always believed, loved her far more than any of us.

Betty and I became great friends of them both and frequently stayed with them. Louise rented a house for shooting or racing, where she entertained lavishly while Boy wrote a book and busied himself with the manufacture of explosive of a very high order.

One evening Louise rang me up while I happened to be stationed in London, suggesting that I drive down to a house she had rented for the shooting season and stay a few days, for there were plenty of pheasants. I was delighted for I was very fond of her. Never would I have found the house without her, for it was deep in beech woods, in a fold of the South Downs. The house, she told me, was very old. For centuries it had belonged to one family, the last of whom had recently died. The autumn colouring was wonderful and in the far distance I could see the sea. My room was at the top of the curving stairs; opposite me was a young American, the head of the younger generation of the Du Pont family, the great arms manufacturers in the State of Delaware. He was excellent company, now on his way home after a tour of European arms and explosive companies. The house was not large but was filled with priceless treasures, which I hardly noticed for as usual Louise had a delightful house-party. The shooting was excellent, fast strong-flying high birds – all wild. My companions were good shots, though Boy was very erratic. I could not have enjoyed it more.

Every night when I finally reached my room I was dead asleep in a moment. The last evening, as I went upstairs, Boy called to me, saying, 'Bob, whatever you may hear, pay no attention, it's only this old house creaking.' Curious, I thought, but I had noticed Boy was not very steady on his feet. Louise waved and up I went with young Du Pont. The moon was full and the valley was as light as day, dozens of owls were hooting at each other.

I awoke at one o'clock, the owls had gone to sleep and there was not a sound in the house or the valley. I felt uneasy. I could not think why. I was wide awake, incapable of movement. I just could not move hand or foot. Slowly and laboriously I sensed at least two men, obviously carrying a heavy load, mounting the stairs. I knew that they were coming to my room and I just lay there spell-bound. The door opened soundlessly. I knew they were within a few feet of me, but I could see nothing. They appeared to cross the room and go out on to the veranda, dumping their load over the railing. They then returned noiselessly the way they had come. No word was spoken. I was not in the least frightened but somewhat horrified, especially when the owls started hooting again. Walking across to Du Pont I asked him if he had heard anything. As it never struck me that what I had experienced was somewhat unusual, I told him what I had heard. He came back with me, looked over the verandah railing; there was of course nothing to be seen. 'I think we all drank too much champagne at dinner, certainly Boy did,' he said and off he went. I thought nothing more about it. I could see no footprints on my carpet but I felt relieved that I did not have to spend another night in that room.

Before lunch Louise found me and said she wanted to show me the garden. We came to a small lawn, beautifully mown, enclosed on three sides by high brick walls. 'Bob, dear,' she said. 'I want to explain to you what you saw last night for that is why Boy and I are not going to buy this old house, and why we sleep in the wing. You see, the house is haunted, there are no two ways about it. In days long ago there were two brothers in the family. The elder inherited the house and lands, the younger coveted them. He engaged a well known swindler and excellent swordsman and they played cards. His elder brother soon realised that he was being cheated, throwing down his cards, he 'called out' the swindler. On this lawn on a night of full moon, the swindler killed him with ease. They then carried him up the stairs, through your room, and tossed his body over the verandah railing. The corpse fell with crash, breaking its neck. The story is well known but few have experienced what you have. I fancy there is a reason for this, for I feel it will form a tie between us. I am going to need your help, Bob, for I cannot live with Boy any more.'

I pondered over all this, keeping most of it to myself. Things went from bad to worse. Louise needed help, and when I offered it, she refused point blank; why I never knew. The whole affair was soon driven out of my mind.

In the spring of 1938, Wilfred Lyde, a trainer at Middleham, told me of a nice sort of horse, called Distant Horizon, well bred and a good jumper, which he thought could well win me another Gold Cup in April. He was expensive but I purchased him, ran him at Carlisle and then at Sandown Park, where he won me my second RA Gold Cup. Peter Bell from Northumberland bought him from me.

The threat of war was looming, it was becoming a certainty. Every time I visited the War Office, asking to be re-posted to 3rd RHA, now in Egypt, I was bemused with offers of a single battery in Penang, the Hong Kong Levies and goodness knows what. In the end they had agreed to post me back to 3rd RHA after Christmas 1937. I liked my territorials, we very nearly won the King's Cup at Larkhill, but if war was to come, I had to be back with my regiment.

Munich came, the war was postponed for a year, preparations began in earnest. In early November, we left our charming little house, all the furniture, less baggage we had ear-marked for Egypt, was sent into store. I had my last day's shooting at Barrack Park while Betty swept the house down from top to toe. We were sad at leaving all our friends, especially the three Irwin sisters. I fell in love with Mary, the eldest, and remained so until she died; Di's bridesmaid fell in love with me, and we both loved and still do, the youngest, Sue, then aged fifteen years old. Mary and Sue frequently stayed with us when it was too late for them to go home. We felt an era had finished; how right it proved.

Chapter 9

PALESTINE

We sailed from England in an old trooper in bitterly cold weather a couple of days after Christmas. The adjutant of 3rd RHA met us on the quayside at Alexandria, directing me to go straight on to Palestine, where 'M' Battery was stationed. Betty went back to Cairo with him, intending to find a flat for us, in which she was most successful.

I was enthralled with Palestine; all the ancient things in Jerusalem fascinated me. The small number of British troops were in Palestine to try and keep the peace between Jew and Arab, vastly outnumbered; it was a difficult role. I took part in the 44th successful entry into Jerusalem. We spent the night in the same spot, an ancient church six miles from the city, as did the Romans. The wounded centurion who died that night before their entry into the city still lies in his leaden sarcophagus in the aisle of the church, down which runs a stream of sweet water. My personal sympathies were with the Arabs, although they proved to be our dangerous enemies. As the spring arrived all those bleak hills became covered with flowers, myriads of scarlet cyclamen appeared in every ancient graveyard. I met Wingate, whom I did not care for; he persuaded me to lie up for a well known Arab bandit one bitterly cold night. Everyone knew we were there so the bandit wisely stayed at home. One day I took a section of our most excellent little howitzers to Nablus with a small escort, where they needed ammunition of all sorts.

On our way back to Lydda across country, we were ambushed by some Arabs from a hilltop village. Foolishly, I had not kept a single round for the howitzers. The Arab rifle fire was heavy but fortunately inaccurate. It dawned on me that unless I did something pretty quickly, I might lose the guns, an unheard of disgrace for a Horse Artillery officer. Our rifle fire was no better than the Arabs', who were completely invisible, firing through chinks in the stone walls, so with every man yelling his head off, we charged up the steep terraced hill. On arrival at the top, there wasn't a man or a rifle to be seen. It took us some time to round up about twenty men whom we took off with us, but we never got a single rifle. I was never caught like that again, my limbers were always full of shells and every man had a hundred rounds of rifle bullets. It was a near thing.

'M' Battery Headquarters were on the edge of Lydda, a small village near the only aerodrome in Palestine. The men lived comfortably on the first floor of the village school and the guns were housed below. The officers' mess was in a small stone-built house opposite. We wired round the football ground to keep out the village livestock. Every afternoon all the flocks were sent there, accompanied by a dozen little boys, who as night fell infiltrated into the outbuildings of the school and stole everything they could put their hands on. They even stole a howitzer shell, goodness knows how. One afternoon Paul Hobbs and I, determined to put an end to this once and for all, tried to round up about a hundred sheep and goats. We failed completely. The more we drove them, the more they circled round behind us. All the little boys yelled with laughter, so we caught six of them and told them to get every animal into a sort of yard adjoining the mess. They did this with ease as all the animals meekly followed them. Paul and I then shut the ancient wooden doors and left them there for the night, including the six small boys. We were covered in fleas.

Next morning, the headmen of the village arrived, escorted by a horde of women wailing and crying. They said that they had no milk for their babies, who would all die – absolute rubbish from the look of the heavy-breasted women. I agreed to release them all provided the headmen gave the six small boys a beating. This they did with gusto. Now, turning to the headmen I said, 'I will not beat you, though you deserve it, instead you will clean out that yard.' Much against their will, they did it and made a good job of it, but they did not like it, as they considered this as women's work.

A few nights later, while I was in my bath, I heard a man calling in the road at the entrance to the mess. Seizing a towel and my revolver, I went out and there was an Arab on the other side of the road, with a rifle, only a few yards away. He had ten shots at me while I shot back at him. I was untouched, so was he. Sadly, he shook his rifle; most of his bullets fell out of it on to the road. Having saluted me, he went off. Just in case another of his ilk arrived, I had the entrance closed with sandbags, a Lewis gun put under my bed and I purchased a charming boxer puppy to sleep on my bed and give me warning of any more hopeful intruders.

The puppy was so cat-mad that I was for ever searching the village for him at night, so I gave him to Betty when she was staying at the King David Hotel in Jerusalem. She adored him and he lived happily for years.

Persistently they tried again, some fifty Arabs woke everyone up by firing at the school from the adjoining graveyard. The men enjoyed it enormously, so did I. Nobody was hit in the battle which went on for about an hour, making a tremendous noise in the silence of the night. Next morning to my chagrin and amazement, not a drop of blood or a corpse was to be found in the graveyard.

Life now returned to its pleasant routine and we managed to carry out some training. The only unpleasant duty, at which we had to take our turn, was accompanying the engine of the train from Jaffa to Jerusalem. The Arabs were always putting pretty heavy home-made bombs under one of the sleepers. I travelled in the cab and four keen-eyed gunners hung on to the footplates, peering ahead. We stopped for 'elevenses', lunch and many alarms, but we did reach Jerusalem each time intact. It was not a pleasant pastime.

Then suddenly we were ordered to return to Cairo by road at once. Betty came down from Jerusalem, gave me Buster, the boxer, flying off to Cairo from Lydda, where she had already installed herself in a charming flat in Gezira.

The real war was drawing nearer.

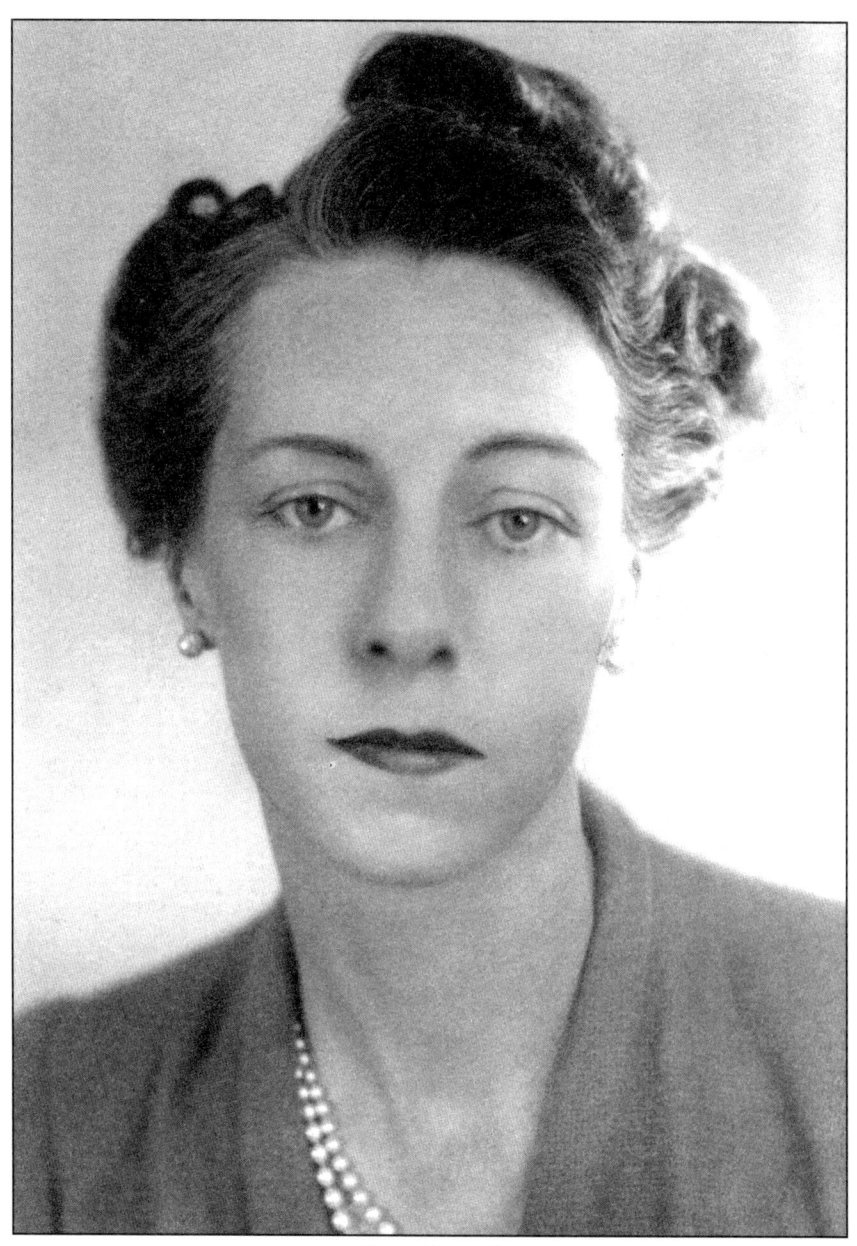

Betty Daniell

Chapter 10

THE WESTERN DESERT CAMPAIGN

I speak of the events of war.
I have not ventured to speak from any chance information, nor
according to any notion of my own.
I have described nothing but what I saw myself, nor any battle in
which I did not fight.

Thucydides
Peloponnesian War, 400 BC

In the following pages, I have not veered from the inspiration of this
wonderful quotation.

Away and away as far as the eye could see, stretched the Western Desert, completely featureless, stony and hard going for the most part, with the occasional large patches of soft powder sand. In one place lay the petrified forest, where in days of long ago, when the whole area was fertile and grew corn for the Mediterranean world, the land was shaded with enormous trees. Then the sea came in, flooding it to a depth of a few feet. As the years went by, the land dried out, the part of these trees under the water absorbed the salt and turned to stone. A mighty storm struck the forest and down came every tree, where they lie to this day.

Very boring it looked and by no stretch of imagination could I believe that for four years I would live out there, with every day a different hazard. How could anyone foretell that I would fight the length of it, across Libya, Tripolitania, through the Mareth Line, into Tunisia to the shores of the Mediterranean Sea.

Then back to England, yet soon off again to Normandy, on across the Seine, by-passing Paris for the benefit of General de Gaulle, to Brussels, Antwerp, through Holland in ghastly winter weather, then as the spring arrived with every hedge a mass of flowering lilac, past the great farms of the Rhineland, each with its nesting storks, we raced the Russians to Lübeck on the Baltic. For the first part of this mammoth journey, we led the 8th Army with the 7th Armoured Division, and for the second part, we led the 2nd Army across Europe with the 11th Armoured Division. Quite a long way from the Nile!

The British troops in Egypt, though very small in number, were commanded by the gallant and stoical General Wavell, who refused to be panicked at any time. The 7th Armoured Division was busy mobilising. I found myself promoted to major, ordered to prepare 'M' Battery for immediate war, retraining all my gunners into their anti-tank role. We were armed with beautiful little 2-pounder anti-tank guns, produced at the Skoda works, which my great grandfather, Sir Richard Griffith once owned. Six thousand rounds was all the ammunition there was in Egypt; it proved enough for sadly these little guns were useless against the big tanks that were to come. When they did come, even George Gun who stoically sat firing, with the help of his sergeant, until their truck was burnt beneath them, died in vain. He was decorated with a posthumous Victoria Cross.

After a few false starts, Mussolini decided to wipe out the 7th Armoured Division, advance in triumph to Cairo, with a ceremonial entry on his beautiful white stallion, which he sent over to Tripoli. Unfortunately for his plans, he had forgotten that the cream of his regular army was in Ethiopia from where they had no means of returning.

I was sitting up on the escarpment, overlooking Sollum with Straffer Gott when the great Italian advance started. The famous Bersaglieri Regiment led the advance; they prudently halted at the frontier wire, but not so their gallant regimental sergeant major who, mounted on a motor-cycle, kept going over the stony waste, all his plumes flying in the wind, until his sword caught in the back wheel and down he came. I walked over and picked him up, turned him round and said, 'arrivederci'. He was equally polite, though I thought somewhat crestfallen.

We slowly withdrew for sixty miles. The Italian Army halted just east of Sidi Barrani, where they built themselves three strongly defended camps. Maktilla was on the seashore, the other two high above on the escarpment.

The Battle of Sidi Barrani, January 1941

General Wavell gave them plenty of time to settle in and to make the track from Sollum into a first class road. Then with the utmost secrecy, he prepared to eliminate them. This he accomplished with a brilliant three pronged dawn attack. I had a number of guns in support of the Coldstream Guards. In the middle of the night we opened fire with everything we had on to the Maktila Camp. By good luck our shells set fire to a number of lorries, which lit up the sky. Everything then was easy. All the Italian soldiers ran about all over the

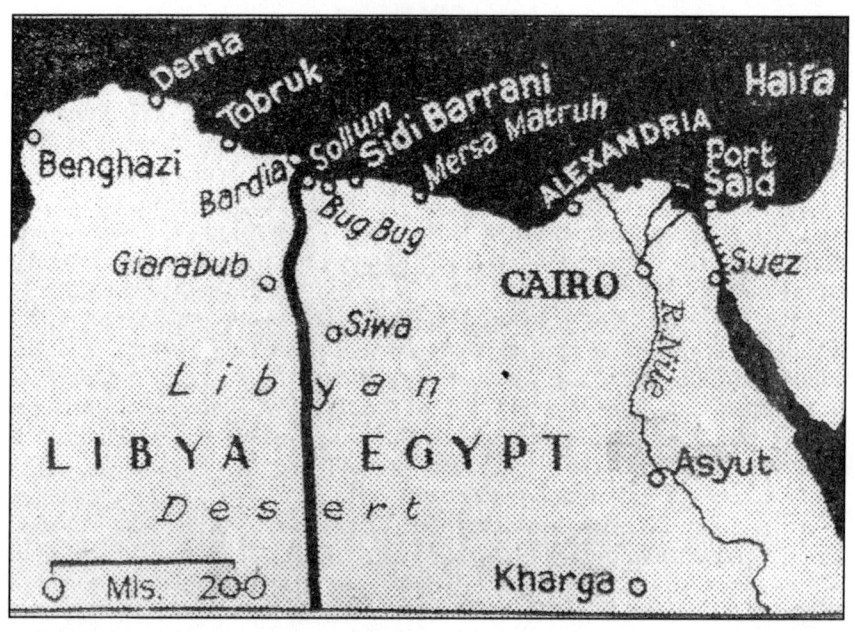
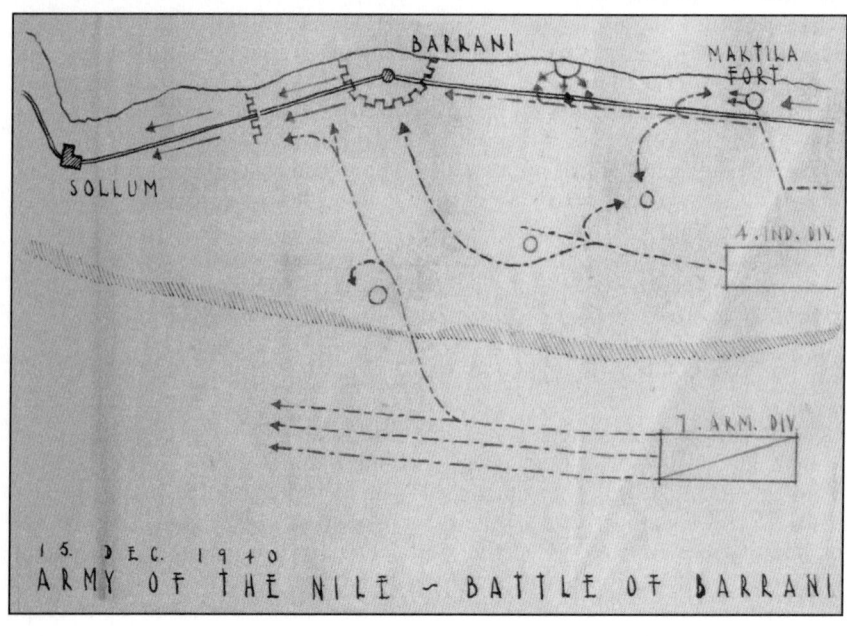

camp, which was in chaos. A few fifteen inch shells from the Queen Elizabeth roared over, bursting with a terrifying noise. Half of the Italian force was composed of Senussi, normally very tough fighters, but they disappeared into the night and were never seen again. At dawn, the remaining two camps were over-run in spite of the bravery of the black-shirt General Maletti, who, seizing a rifle, attacked a tank of the 7th Hussars, single handed, much to the astonishment of the tank crew. The whole Italian army of 35,000 soldiers then threw down their arms and surrendered. That was the Battle of Sidi Barrani.

I was suffering very badly from vicious desert sores with both my hands in an old pair of stockings. This did not prevent me dashing about all over the Maktila Camp, looking for mementoes. I did not find much, except a charming old Italian general who gave me his card and asked me if I could give him a cup of coffee. His name was Generalissimo Gallina. I handed him over to a budding young staff captain, for I was really looking for revolvers and cameras.

There were many really beautiful dogs wandering about, thoroughly deranged by the shelling. I picked up a nice little corgi-type dog, who, having bitten me through the wrist, settled down very comfortably. I could not have done a more stupid thing, for in a few days time, he developed rabies and subsequently bit nineteen men. I was having treatment for my desert sores and did not hear of this for some two weeks. I immediately flew down to Cairo from Mersa Matruh to consult the Pasteur Clinic. Two very pleasant elderly Belgian professors listened to my tale, they told me that regretfully there was nothing they could do for me, as I was long over the time limit for the effectiveness of their serum. They hoped my death would occur shortly so that I should not be worried too unduly! Thanking them, I said I wished to live a long time, as I had much to do and requested a fourteen-day period of daily double doses. They agreed reluctantly. Bolstered up by Betty and a daily half bottle of champagne, I survived, though definitely apprehensive of what might come. By a miracle, the dog had bitten me through the worst of my desert sores; this undoubtedly saved me, one bug killing the other.

Betty and I thoroughly enjoyed our few days together in our most comfortable flat. This was abruptly terminated by a young staff captain who appeared and said I was to go at once to Ismailia and take charge of a gunner regiment which slept all day and by night lined the banks of the Suez Canal, endeavouring to shoot down the heavy German planes which, flying very low, dropped enormous mines into the rocky stretch of the canal, thereby closing it.

After a very pleasant restful week of this, orders came through to collect all the men, fit them out with thick battle dress and join a small force which was destined to capture Rhodes, erroneously believed not to be occupied by the Germans. Very fortunately for me, Rommel made his appearance in the desert, frightening the wits out of everyone with his amazingly rapid advances and the extreme destructiveness of his heavy tanks.

Again a breathless young captain arrived, with orders for me to drop everything, report as second in command to a territorial regiment, the South Notts Hussars, who had recently arrived in the country. He said I would find this regiment, with any luck, somewhere in the Tell-el-Kebir area, about thirty miles west of Ismailia. I was then to lead them at once to Tobruk, some five hundred to six hundred miles away. By the time we had arrived at Sollum, I had got to know them a little, an excellent lot of men and NCOs. The regiment was commanded by the local Master of Foxhounds.

Chapter 11

THE TEN-MONTH SIEGE OF TOBRUK AND
THE BATTLE OF THE CAULDRON

In March 1941 time was crucial and three hundred lorries were waiting to join my convoy at Sollum. Tobruk was obviously under heavy attack but I found the Padre, Parry, a very argumentative Welsh rugger international, brewing up his tea. I exploded and we got under way; as it grew dark, I ordered every vehicle to put on their head-lights, an unheard of procedure in the desert. However it worked, five hundred head-lights coming steadily on, frightened off the few Germans blocking the road and we entered Tobruk. There we remained for the next ten months, in company with the Australian 6th Division, three other gunner regiments and a heavy anti-aircraft battery. Tobruk in other circumstances could have been a charming place: a narrow deep anchorage, half a dozen white-washed cottages, with a deep and rocky seaboard. As it turned out, it was very boring, our rations were basic and dull beyond words, the seaboard was exceedingly dangerous, you dived into deep clear cool water, but getting out again was difficult owing to the outward tow.

Every morning at ten o'clock and again at four a dozen or so German Junkers dive-bombers arrived from Crete, bombing the harbour and the gun positions, ending always with an accurate machine gunning of everything that moved. On our arrival there was not even a cemetery. By the time the seige was over, there it was with over one thousand white crosses silhouetted against the deep blue sea.

John Weller-Poley signalled that he would like to be posted to me; a charming very good-looking young man, he was our first reinforcement to 'M' Battery, straight from Cambridge. He and I had become great friends, so it could not have been nicer to see him again and hear the news of the war, now two hundred miles east of Tobruk.

As the days went by, I collected all the Italian guns lying about, some fifty of them serviceable, all made by Vickers. There was plenty of their ammunition, so we fired them until they burst, thus saving our 25-pounders, whose ammunition was scanty. Betty, from Alexandria, with great ingenuity filled a kerosene oil tin with whisky, tinned fruit, underclothes, socks, shoes, chocolate

91

and cigarettes, sealed it, describing its contents as nails. She then charmed one of the two officers of the two very gallant Australian destroyers to deliver it to me on his next run, until they were both torpedoed. They made the run to Tobruk on four pitch dark nights each month. How welcome they were!

Parry, the padre, came to me and said he wished to hold a service on Sunday evenings. I replied, 'Find a place underground, padre, and I will help you all I can.' Off he went, fuming, and found an ancient bier, or rock cave, hollowed out centuries ago where the Bedouin stored their wheat, a narrow entrance closed with a stone. Here this amazing man held his services, lit by resin flares, attended to capacity by about six hundred men every Sunday night. The Reverend Parry was a very brave man. I have absolutely no doubt that he feared death and mutilation, like any other soldier, yet whenever I arrived at a gun position in the throes of a savage dive-bomb attack, there he was already, inspiring the gunners by his calm and welcome presence.

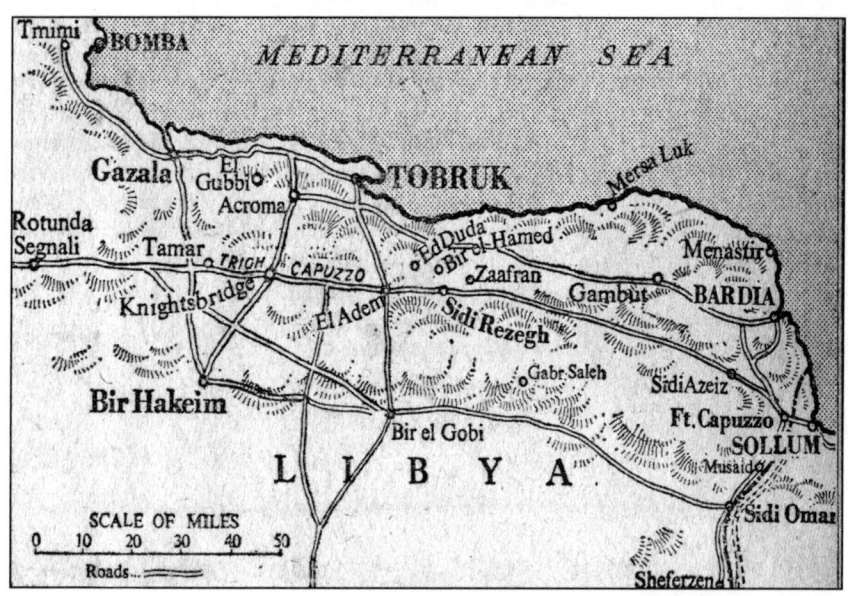

The Germans left the siege of Tobruk to the Italian army and the dive-bombers, while they advanced some hundred miles to Sollum. Suddenly we got a signal from Cairo to the effect that a Panzer Division was preparing to attack Tobruk in the next two days. Early in the morning, the German tanks arrived, exactly where we had been told to expect them, followed by endless columns of lorried infantry. We could not stop the tanks, though only a few penetrated the perimeter, but four regiments of 25-pounders, firing all out until the barrels of the guns got white hot, very successfully dealt with the lorried German infantry. As evening drew on, all was quiet again. Our doctor and I went up to the anti-tank ditch, completely filled with the dead and dying young Germans. We gave them what water we had brought with us but, when one of them had a shot at the doctor, we left them to their own devices.

One of their new Mark IV tanks had meandered across the waste land inside the perimeter early in the afternoon. As it approached our regimental headquarters, one of the driving tracks just broke. The young crew jumped out, dismayed beyond words, for they were all alone, there was no fight left in them. I walked over to them, directing them towards the rear, where no doubt someone would pick them up. I then climbed into the tank, it was absolutely brand new and smelled as if it had just come out of the workshops. I noted that the gun was a short 75mm, new to the desert and very powerful. I took an excellent photograph of it and sent it back to headquarters in Cairo. I suppose there was little they could do about it, for the next two attempts to relieve Tobruk were quickly halted by these guns. Later that evening, Padre Parry set that tank on fire. He said that he did not like German tanks.

Eventually Tobruk was relieved; there was a fierce engagement at Sidi Resagh, a few miles south. Jock Campbell and George Gun earned two good VCs. I know nothing of it, as I was not there. The German armour for reasons best known to themselves, now retired to the west. As I drove out to watch the Germans withdrawing up along the Broad Track, known as the Trig, I saw a staff car driving straight towards me. I stopped it by firing a few rounds into the air, for it might well have held Germans. Out stepped Alan Moorehead, whom I had met once during the siege.

On his return to Cairo, he had gone to see Betty and described to her the small sandbagged igloo in which I lived. He said I wanted to be the first man to enter Tobruk from the desert. I pointed out to him the columns of dust along the Trig, warning him that they were Rommel's armour withdrawing. He wouldn't believe me as he was convinced they were New Zealanders. On his way back from the headquarters in Tobruk, he drove straight into the columns and was taken prisoner. I hurried across the Trig to look for Sidney de Salis' body, for his wife's sake. I knew he had been in the engagement at Sidi Resagh but I could only find his overcoat. It transpired he had been taken prisoner. On the way back I picked up half a dozen lorries of New Zealanders who were lost. One was full of loaves of bread; they gave me a few and how good they were after ten months of army biscuits!

Betty and many other army wives were VADs in the 15th British Hospital in Cairo. What a delight they must have been to everyone, except the matron!

Generals came and generals went, though I seldom saw them. Straffer Gott was shot down late one evening and killed. Jock Campbell turned over in his car and broke his neck. Ritchie, whom we knew well in Palestine, with his marvellous blue eyes, was in command for a short period, followed by

Cunningham, a charming man, always with a smile. Now it was Auchinleck and, though he did not know it, his days were numbered. The fighting trailed backwards and forwards along the desert, parallel to the coast, always leaving behind it the ghastly toll of dead men, blown up on mines, burnt to a cinder in tanks, smashed to pieces by the Italian heavy bombers, and riddled by the German Mark IV tank heavy machine guns.

Rommel was a great leader, beloved by his men. He was always to be found where the fighting was fiercest. He walked into an Italian casualty clearing station once and noticed some British wounded who quite obviously had not been attended to. He sent for the senior medical officer and had him arrested, telling him that all wounded soldiers were alike, whatever their nationality. The men of the German Afrika Korps were excellent fighters, all young, intelligent and spotlessly clean. Unlike the British soldiers, they were apt to lose heart very easily when things went wrong. The vast distances of the desert worried them; the fear of getting lost was ever with them.

When all our aeroplanes had been shot down, mostly by German ME 109s, we suffered severely from the Italian high level heavy bombers. Watching them coming over, you could count the bombs dropping and, as long as you could do this, you knew that you would be safe, for they would all explode behind you.

Rommel had four of our 25-pounder guns with him at his headquarters. He thought they were excellent guns but not as useful as his 88mm guns. A young subaltern of mine, who was taken prisoner, was in charge of them. He took a very good snapshot of Rommel which he gave me when, in a chaotic mix-up at dusk, I happened to rescue him and some fifteen other men.

It was winter time now in 1941 and occasionally there were periods of heavy rain, making huge shallow lakes, where thousands and thousands of wild duck rested. Goodness knows where they came from. They were on their way north to Europe. At night their flight overhead was thunderous. I shot some succulent young gazelle one early morning and saw the pug-marks of a cheetah clearly marked in the mud on the edge of one of these lakes, so they were not completely extinct.

Christmas 1941 came – what a long year it had been. As Tobruk was now no longer threatened by Italians or Germans, I handed my guns over to a Polish regiment and left the 107th South Notts Hussars to find their own way back to Cairo, which they accomplished in record time.

While the regiment was refitting and retraining with three new territorial tank regiments, I stayed happily with Betty, revelling in a hot bath at night, a comfortable bed and clean uniform. At the end of a month, we were off again to finish our training south of Tobruk. On paper our 22nd Armoured Brigade was strong in tanks, guns and men but at the full moon at the end of April, when Rommel advanced again with his 21st and 15th Panzer regiments, all now equipped with their Mark IV tanks, supported by infantry, we were very quickly disillusioned. Our tank regiments were utterly destroyed, in spite of the heroic

Rommel

support of our guns, for no 25-pounder is much good against heavily armoured tanks and our anti-tank guns were only 2-pounders. I was with a troop of four 25-pounders under the command of Captain Bennett. We were watching the last of the Churchill tanks going up in flames, when four Mark IV German tanks came straight for the guns. One of the tanks suffered a direct hit at a range of under a hundred yards, killing the crew; with flames belching from the turret, an awesome sight, on it came, straight into the gun. In the meantime, the other three opened up with their heavy machine guns, piercing the gun shields like brown paper, killing most of the gun crews. Beside me, out of the corner of my eye, I saw Padre Parry, hauling a couple of wounded into the back of his truck. I shouted to him to leave. Just in time he disappeared, six wounded in the truck and four bullets in Padre Parry. Exhorting his driver to go faster, yet faster, they eventually reached safety. Parry survived for a few years. Captain Bennett, a couple of his men and I lay as dead. With great relief, we saw the tanks pass us by. Exciting but somewhat nerve-racking!

For two weeks the British armoured brigades fought a losing battle, but the Germans were held. Our defence was much assisted by the Scots Guards and a few guns entrenched on the edge of the escarpment, a safe anchorage named Knightsbridge. Then came two days of a violent dust-storm, called Hamseen. Nothing could move while it lasted. Suddenly the Germans gathered their scattered units together and withdrew westwards to their forward base at the Rotunda. I fancy they were out of petrol. We too collected what was left of our men and guns, a pitiful remnant of the strong brigade of so short a time ago. I do not know what our brigadier thought of it all for I never saw him. He was a charming man with a pleasant voice and lived in a lovely old red-brick house in Norfolk near Bungay.

Late one night I got a wireless message to collect every man and gun that I could find and rendezvous at a spot half-way down the Gazala-Bir Hachem minefield next evening (there were no mines). There Herbert Lumsden, who was commanding what remained of the armoured brigades, met us. I was very glad to see him, for we had ridden in many steeplechases together. He said that he wanted my support group to go forward when the moon rose about 1 a.m., following in the wake of the German armour to the Rotunda. If they had refuelled and left the place, we were to destroy everything there. At that moment we were heavily and accurately dive-bombed, trucks blew up, several officers were killed including General Lumsden's intelligence officer. The general was visibly shaken; as he drove off he said, 'I want you to put down fifty rounds a gun about 9 a.m. to discourage any German movement northwards.'

The Cauldron, 1st to 3rd June 1942

We had a meal, dumped fifty rounds per gun for this perfectly pointless barrage, then we threw away every surplus piece of equipment from the trucks and filled up with extra water and rations. Had we only known what was to come, it was a useless pastime for within forty-eight hours, 90% of the men were dead and all the guns destroyed or captured. As the moon rose, we moved off in the now dead silent night; by dawn we were well on our way but, when topping a rise, we were met with a hail of shells. We dropped into action where we were, on a horrible stony ridge, which proved our undoing. Behind us was a large bowl, so now this disastrous one-sided engagement is called 'The Cauldron'. More and more German tanks appeared until they had totally surrounded us, standing off at a safe distance, while their guns proceeded to pound every vehicle to pieces. Our casualties became very heavy; we could not move, as my orders were precise – 'to stand and fight where we were to the last man and the last round'.

During the night, elements of an Indian infantry brigade moved up into the bowl behind us; they had a lot of guns but not a single round of ammunition, as all their supply lorries were lost. Their brigadier was lost or killed. Another Indian battalion went forward to the next ridge, where they were annihilated to a man, followed by a very brave Scottish battalion who, I fear, shared their fate, for I never saw one of them again.

Just before dawn, I got through to Brigadier Carr. I told him the situation was untenable, but I thought, with the help of all my smoke shells, I could get the wounded out, most of the guns and what few men remained. He repeated his previous orders, most emphatically, so, being a regular officer, I did as I was told. For the next two days, the situation was unchanged with the casualties mounting hourly. The German tanks moved in closer and closer, eliminating all the Indian positions with ease, as they had no mines or anti-tank guns. On the last afternoon, I was so tired, I lay down by the sole remaining gun. I woke up suddenly to find a German staff car beside me, two generals behind with a staff officer in front. Leaping on to the running board, I ordered them out as prisoners. Like a flash, the staff officer hit me across the eyes with his map case. The car swerved round and drove off at speed. I missed it with the last two rounds from the 25-pounder.

The end came slowly but surely, all the vehicles were burning, all the charges exploding under the heavy machine gun fire. I walked across to a gun that seemed to be still intact. At that moment a Mark IV appeared out of the smoke at point blank range. A dejected looking gunner loaded it for me. I could not miss and up went that German tank with a violent explosion. It was still there six months later when I returned to the Cauldron after Alamein. Immediately one of their small but powerful assault guns knocked out my gun. I had been seen, the machine gun fire was very heavy, so I lay down and started to roll into the smoke of a burning vehicle. The German infantry were now all over the position. I knew that in an hour it would be pitch dark, but so did they.

The awful noise of battle ceased completely. A solitary lark flew up into the sunset sky. I prayed for a miracle and my prayer was answered. Untouched, I walked over to my 8-cwt truck; Dr Saunders with whom I had lived every day for two years, would not accompany me. I was a Horse Artillery man and the Horse Artillery never surrender, so I drove off at speed towards four Mark IVs. That foxed them for a short time; they missed me and I was clear. Not for very long, however, for there in front of me was a long line of lorries filled with the German 90 Light Division. I had to accompany them. As soon as I saw a chance I turned south for the open desert, only to have all four wheels of my truck blown off by an 88mm.

A German sergeant shouted to me to join his post. He could so easily have killed me but he didn't; he let me walk off with my water bottle. I blessed him, for it was now dark and I knew I had many miles to go. Gerald Grosvenor picked me up in his tank, several days later, by which time I was in very poor shape, virtually the only one to escape from the Battle of the Cauldron, where the South Notts Hussars with the brave men who supported them, fought so well and truly to the 'last man and the last round'.

The author in the desert

Chapter 12

RETREAT

General Lumsden had his headquarters at El Adem, so I dropped in there to give him the news of the disastrous Battle of the Cauldron. He found it hard to believe. He asked me if I would like to take over all the South African guns now in Tobruk. I thanked him but declined, then hurried back to where my supply vehicles were bivouacked, had a bath, found a clean uniform and set off at once for Cairo. I told the regimental sergeant major to make a battery out of what men he had and send four lorries with spare drivers straight to Cairo.

He was to withdraw slowly down the coast road, keeping twenty miles ahead of any Germans. On arrival at about 1 a.m., I woke up Brigadier Maxwell. I don't think he really believed things were as bad as I said. However, having promoted me to lieutenant-colonel, he gave me carte blanche to take any 25-pounders I could find. I only found four. As soon as my lorries arrived, I hitched the guns on to the back and sent them straight off again. It nearly killed the drivers, but they went. I met Paul Hobbs who was also on his way back. I told him what had happened; he stole a lorry and, driving to the hospital, shouted for any men of 3rd RHA who could walk to come with him. Fourteen pyjama-clad figures appeared and jumped into the lorry.

For thirty-six hours I slept and rested with Betty at our flat. We had dinner together, long candles on the table, Betty in a white dress and diamonds, myself in my white dinner jacket. The night was very dark, there was not a sound from the usually noisy bazaar, so no doubt the bad news from the desert had reached the city. Betty had refused to be evacuated to South Africa, until I was dead, but she must have been wondering, as we drank our champagne, how much longer it would be before this happened. I left next morning and found a very small force holding out on the Ruiuriset Ridge, a long long way east of Tobruk. Here the flies were more troublesome than the Germans – they were unbelievably awful.

Some days later I was flown to Cairo to tell the story of the Battle of the Cauldron before a court of enquiry under General Jumbo Wilson, as president, with ten general officers as members, especially flown out from England, for the purpose of enquiring into the facts of this disastrous battle with its appalling loss of men and material.

One day a red-capped general drew up in a staff car. He said, 'Are you Major Daniell?'

'Yes,' I replied.

'Well, I want you to show me the German positions. Will you take me round?' I refused and showed him a signal that had just been handed to me, warning all officers of a bogus general, a German, who was touring around and on no account was he to be shown anything. He laughed and said, 'I am General Alexander; don't you know me?' I regretted that I had never seen him before in my life, though his face seemed familiar. 'Well,' he said, 'I always give the Irish Guards shamrock on St Patrick's Day.' Then I remembered him.

It was very hot in the afternoon, an excellent moment to move pretty close to the Germans. We were sitting on the edge of a slit-trench, when General Alexander turned to me, saying, 'Something is moving at the bottom of this trench under my feet.'

'Don't worry, General,' I said, 'that is one of the Punjabis on look-out; they always sleep in the afternoon.' After a couple of weeks on this noisome ridge, where the dead still lay around unburied owing to the solid rock, we were ordered to move back a few miles to a prepared position at a spot named Hahem al Haffa. Here, General Freyberg, commanding the New Zealanders, flatly refused to move back another yard. Anyway, General Montgomery arrived, revitalising everyone in a few hours, so we stopped where we were.

On the way back one evening, I had collected a motley crowd of weary soldiers. We were sitting around in a patch of soft sand, when there appeared one of our Hurricane planes, flying very low in obvious trouble. I had not seen a British plane for months. Sure enough, a German ME109 dropped out of the sky. We had a Bofors gun with us, so for a time we could keep him away. Alas our ammunition was soon expended. That was the end of the Hurricane. I think the pilot was dead before he hit the ground. The 109 was also hit and burning. The German pilot landed by parachute among us. He was very truculent, wanting all sorts of things. I could not be bothered with him. I told him to go and bury the pilot of the Hurricane.

Before we settled down in what became the Alamein line, the Germans made one last most determined attack. About thirty tanks and a horde of lorried infantry appeared. The 44th Division straight out from England gave the latter a terrible hammering, stopping them completely. The tanks came on alone; they were nearly all hit and left burning by a handful of our tanks who, digging themselves in among the sandy hillocks were quite invisible. All very satisfactory. A South African sergeant beckoned me over and we split a bottle of South African brandy and chatted about Cape Town.

When we heard this attack was imminent, the result looked doubtful to me, so I sent my staff-car back to Cairo with instructions to obtain all the petrol they could carry from a thoroughly dishonest garage owner whom I knew. If the Germans reached the Alexandria to Cairo road, they were to drive Betty south to Aswan, where she could get a felucca on to Wadi Halfa and safety. I intended to withdraw slowly into Palestine. Thanks to General Montgomery, all this became unnecessary.

The weeks went by. General Montgomery was in no hurry. He knew that the long line of the German communications was a serious hazard for them. However, as October started, I could feel things were moving. The 23rd October was full moon, so on the 20th I drove back to Alexandria, had my hair cut at the Palace Hotel, and purchased from the barman for 30 shillings three of the best wrist watches (undoubtedly stolen) I have ever had and I still have them.

The Battle of Alamein was fought for many days; it was tough, very tough and very noisy both by day and by night. The armoured brigade to which I was attached had, as its first objective when the guns finally opened fire, to penetrate the huge minefield in the south, thus forcing Rommel to send some of his tanks south. He didn't send many – that minefield was full of mines and heavily defended. It cost us dear both in men and equipment.

We were then ordered north, where we sat for several days in the middle of the German minefield in full view of everyone; fortunately it seemed every man was too busy with his own small battle to worry about us. Eventually the 11th Hussars arrived with a sack of welcome oranges; they hoped to follow us later that evening along the Gamma Track. The guns never stopped pounding away. About 2 a.m. we set off in a long line, travelling westwards. We never saw a German, not a soul fired at us. By dawn we were through, out again into the open desert; oh the relief of it after all those weeks penned up behind the German mine fields !

Brigadier Roberts, who commanded the armoured brigade, was furious with me when I poured some petrol on to the sand and proceeded to brew some tea. I needed some breakfast.

As we approached Fuka, where Rommel himself commanded the German rearguard, all hell was let loose. Several German maniacs ran towards our tanks, apparently attempting to capture them. They had no arms. A few 88mm guns opened up at point blank range. Fortunately they only had a few shells. The young gunners of the Afrika Korps then stood by their guns, refusing to surrender. A couple of captured 25-pounders appeared from my rear. With considerable difficulty, I forced them to stop, for we needed them badly. The main German retreat was along the coast road, a comparatively narrow strip. We were above them on the escarpment, down which there were very few passable tracks. It was our vehicles and tanks which ran out of petrol, much delaying us, with the result that the German main body arrived at Sollum first, getting clean away. They took every vehicle belonging to their allies, the Italians, leaving them to walk. I was very sorry for the thousands of them, stretching away in long lines, with nowhere to go and nothing to drink. In front of us up on the escarpment were several strong detachments of German tanks and their powerful 88mm guns. They fought well but they could not stop the pursuit. Down on the coast road, it was the same story, 3rd RHA were down there with the 4th Armoured Brigade.

Back at last south of Tobruk, we halted for a couple of days for petrol and supplies to reach us. Brigadier Roberts and the 22nd Armoured Brigade went elsewhere. Roscoe Harvey with his 4th Light Armoured Brigade appeared. General Montgomery came up and I met him for the first time. We got on well and he offered me command of my own regiment – 3rd RHA. I was back where I wanted to be and was delighted. Roscoe Harvey and I had ridden in many steeplechases together before the war. We remained together until we reached the Baltic at Lübeck two years later. He was an ideal commander of armour, brave, competent, of iron determination, never rattled even in the most alarming situations and much admired by the men he led. He is today, as then, my best friend.

I took the opportunity to revisit the Cauldron. I was horrified at the heaps of dead still unburied; the Germans seemed only to have stayed there for a day. I imagine they did what they could. I inspected the shattered remains of the tank which I hit with the last shell fired from the position. My notebook was under the large stone where I had left it but I was delighted to see that a large number of 25-pounders had been left there. Without their firing mechanisms, wisely buried in the sand, they were useless to the Germans. It was a silent brooding place. I was glad to leave it to the shifting sands to obliterate the sadness and the futility of it all, and all those brave men who had gone from us for ever.

Engagements with the enemy went on unceasingly. Early in December 1942, General Freyberg and his very pleasant New Zealand Division arrived. We were to lead them south deep into the Sahara, taking ten days hard rations and water, then turning north, thus cutting off the large German force in the Agheila fortified position. Down there the desert was undisturbed, camels and Bedouin just wandering about, until we came to a deep ravine, barring our way. Roscoe, General Freyberg and I clambered down the cliff sides, finding four feet of powder dust at the bottom. There wasn't a vehicle made that could cross that. By a miracle it rained that night; I doubt such a thing had happened since the days of the Roman 9th Legion, who had passed that way to disappear for ever. In the morning the dust had turned to concrete and we crossed with ease.

Some days later, we came across an unknown oasis, clear running water and palm trees, with the ruins of several generations of derelict mud buildings – the first natural water I had seen since the Nile. A lone reconnaissance plane spotted us; this dangerous gamble had just not quite come off, but when we did reach the coast road, we completely destroyed the German rearguard although we ourselves were clean out of petrol. On to Tripoli, captured in a very exciting night attack, through an unmapped pass in the hills. Tripoli was a delightful seaside town, with excellent docks. The Germans had disappeared so I appropriated a delightful villa with a lovely garden overlooking the sea, for a few days rest. A thoroughly undesirable villain cautiously approached me. He offered me the mistress, rather an attractive Italian girl, of the late German commandant. Reluctantly I refused her. However I stood him up against the wall, telling him I required a villa complete with servants and a piano for my officers by eleven o'clock next morning. He was dithering with fear but he did arrange the whole thing.

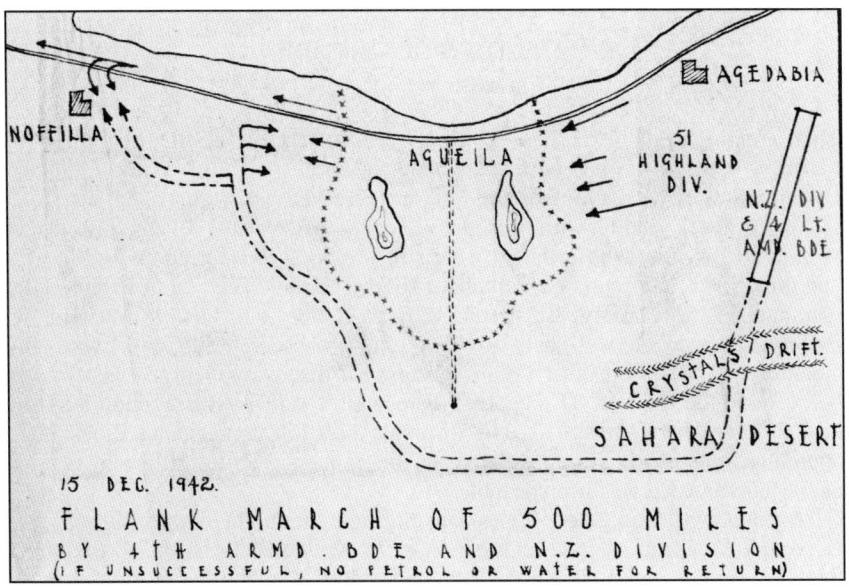

Chapter 13

THE TURN OF THE TIDE

That great man Winston Churchill arrived in Tripoli at the beginning of February 1943 and, on a perfect evening, he took the salute of the Highland Division and certain troops of the 7th Armoured Division along the sea front. He then shook hands with all the commanding officers of the 4th Light Armoured Brigade, whose troops were still watching the German withdrawal. I had three first class battery commanders in 3rd RHA – Terence O'Brien-Butler commanded 'M' Battery, Basil Buckwell 'J' Battery and George Masters 'D' Battery. They were well able to look after themselves and cope with any emergency. I left them to it – they preferred it that way. George Masters was beloved by the men of 'D' Battery; there wasn't a man who wouldn't follow him through the hottest hell. Highly explosive, his language at times quite appalling, he was always considerate of the gunners. He was killed by a mine near Medenine. He was irreplaceable.

A couple of days later, I was woken about midnight with a signal from General John Harding, now commanding 7th Armoured Division, to the effect that, in company with Brigadier Joy and Julian Heathcoat-Amory, I was to reconnoitre the village of Nalut, a very strongly fortified village, 125 miles behind the German lines. I was furious. It was an extremely dangerous undertaking and nothing whatsoever to do with me. If things went wrong, it would be a very long walk back. General Montgomery himself had signed the order, so I just had to go. Setting out in the half-light, we drove up a marvellous road over the hills, 4,000 feet high and then off due west at top speed, along a passable sandy track. Herds of gazelle, grazing peaceably, barely looked up as we passed. It was a lovely day and, had it not been for the anxiety at each bend that we might run into a party of Germans, all would have been idyllic. About 3 p.m., we reached the Gedames crossroads, the old slave route from the south – no sign of the Free French from Lake Chad.

In front of us was a huge rock pile, precipitous cliffs, topped by a small walled village with not a sign of a German. We split up and I ran up a dreadful track to the village. Not a single soul paid the slightest attention to me. In minutes the air force was due to arrive and obliterate the village. I dashed down, rejoined the others, and we drove round and round in a circle to attract their attention. Whether they saw us or not I do not know, they only dropped a few token bombs. I did not feel at all happy in this remote spot and made off at once at a reasonable speed for home. I was nervous, I could not settle down until dusk. Then we pulled off the track and bivouacked in some thick trees. We needed something to eat and there nearby was a large flock of sheep and goats. Could we catch one of the fat lambs? It drove us mad but, at last we got a beauty.

In no time it was roasting, such a marvellous smell and so good to eat. Tired out we all slept like logs. We had been very fortunate for the Germans had only left a couple of hours before we passed. I was still furious as it might so easily have ended in tears.

The Germans withdrew behind the Mareth Line in Tunisia, a strong position, from which they delivered a sudden attack, completely halted by our guns. 'D' Battery lost the lorry carrying their NAAFI supplies; this really did annoy George Masters. Roscoe Harvey brought up some tanks and got through the Mareth Line with a most unexpected attack. On again, there was a very tough encounter at the Wadi Akarit. Away out to sea was the island of Jerba, connected to the mainland by a one and a half mile causeway, well built by the Romans. This island was the home of pirates and a very religious sect. It looked a lovely place with the blue sea all around. In Tunisia, the country changed completely with miles and miles of corn and groves of well-tended olive trees. I was up in the hills with the 4th Light Armoured Brigade, where the ground was completely covered with wild flowers, red, blue, yellow and every colour under the sun. I always chose an area of blue flowers, as I thought it was a lucky colour for me and my headquarters.

Rather a pleasant American colonel attached himself to me and at seven o'clock one morning, on a plain golden with marigolds, there was an historic meeting. Charles Keightley from the 1st Army, an American general from the Kerousin Pass and myself from the 8th Amy. In the distance lay the whitewashed walled city of Kairouan, which I visited later.

At Enfidaville, the Germans blocked the coast road and there was heavy fighting down there; sadly Paul Hobbs was hit by a chance shell and killed outright. We had been together since the days of Palestine. I was shocked by his death so near the end of it all.

High mountains faced us – with no roads or tracks, we could go no further. Some Spahis, most colourful in their scarlet capes and a French Equatorial Artillery Regiment armed with 100/75 guns were attached to me. I fired the lot one morning. I hoped it frightened somebody up in the mountains. Things were moving elsewhere, the 1st Army was stuck at Mejez, with the American army somewhere about. General Horrocks took over the 7th Armoured Division at 10 p.m. on a night of pitch darkness. He ordered the very scattered regiments to move at once, crossing the hills to the west by a narrow pass and to proceed at top speed to join the 1st Army at Mejez-el-Bab. This pass was cut by the Romans and a very fine fort guarded the top. One of my guns went over the precipice, so I halted until dawn. As I ate my breakfast in the fort, a marvellous view stretched away below me, a river winding away from Mejez-el-Bab, pine trees and flocks of birds around, also plenty of those new horrible German personnel mines. My nice doctor trod on one and it took me two hours to get him clear but he did survive.

As we coasted down towards Mejez, the tree-lined roads were lined with dumps of shells, hastily erected marquees marked as casualty clearing stations, with lorries and trucks just parked nose to tail. Obviously the German air force must have been destroyed, as indeed it had been, and undoubtedly there was a battle imminent.

THE LAST BATTLE AT MEDJEZ-EL-BAB, 5th MAY 1943

I brought all my guns into action below the final ridge just beyond the river. Here my brother, Tony, met me, a fantastic chance encounter. Early next morning our tanks came up and over we went, Peter Gregson with the 5th RHA following hard behind. We gained a complete surprise and, almost untouched, we raced north for Tunis. Thousands of German troops had been cut off and were collecting in vast numbers at Pont-de-Fas. As we approached the outskirts of the city of Tunis, I told Charles Armitage, my new second in command, to

German Tiger Tank

take the regiment at all speed west to the river at Portoville and seize the bridge. They were too late, it was blown. A Tiger tank, which I had never seen before, was astride the road with one of its giant tracks broken. I told Charles not to bother with the hundreds of Germans milling about asking to surrender. I turned round and raced into Tunis. I wanted to be the first man into the city. The 11th Hussars say they had that honour, good power to them – they were the best regiment in the 8th Army. The city was in a state of chaos, thousands of Arabs milling around, lots of French showering flowers and kisses. The whole of the Herman Goering Division, with their gilt buttons, threw away their arms in panic; they never fired a shot. Parties of Germans taking refuge in schools, anywhere to escape having their throats cut, which a great number failed to do.

I went to a large house, rang the bell and found it belonged to a French doctor. I said I would like a bath and some lunch. He was delighted and both were very much appreciated. So this was the finish, the end of the campaign. Two thousand miles and three years of fierce daily fighting. I really could hardly believe it: the total surrender of all the German and Italian forces in North Africa.

All along the road to the west from Tunis, stretched gently sloping hills, completely covered with pines. Above where my batteries were bivouacked stood a small white-washed farm. I drove up to it and found a very welcoming French family who invited me to lunch. I stayed there a week. There were two daughters who took great care of me, the younger and more attractive of the two, gave up her room to me. We became firm friends and she wrote to me for several years after the war. They had no petrol, so at least I could drive them to market most days.

On the last Sunday I had a drumhead service, all the guns in a semi-circle, and each battery chose their own hymn. Every man was present, even an agnostic, who told me that he could not attend. I told him I did not care whether he lived or died – he was there alright. General Harding was not with us; he had been wounded somewhere along the coast road, so it was General Horrocks who ordered the whole of the 7th Armoured Division out of Tunis and back to Homs in Libya to bivouac where they pleased. I read out to the men all the congratulatory messages and told them what a good job they had done; not surprisingly, I said, for we are all Horse Artillery men to whom nothing is impossible.

13th MAY, 1943, 2.15 p.m.

General Alexander signalled to Mr Churchill, 'It is my duty to report that the Tunisian campaign is over. All enemy resistance has ceased. We are masters of the North African shores.' Before leaving the area, I lunched with my brother Tony and his very pleasant divisional commander. After lunch we walked down to the gate of the farm, where a huge military policeman was on duty. He watched me get into the staff car, blow the horn, and immediately my faithful little brown hen jumped into the back with all the tools. Just as we drove away, he turned to his general saying, 'Sir, I have heard a lot about the 8th Army; now I have seen it and I still don't believe it!'

Tony went on to Italy, winning a good MC on the Rapido River. I eventually flew back to England under the care of the Americans. Now I wanted to find Paul Hobbs's grave so I left it to my battery commanders to find their own way back to Homs; no one relished this move.

Round Pont-du-Fas, there were hundreds and hundreds of Germans, who had surrendered. They blackened the plain and I could not see anyone looking after them. At Enfidaville, I found Paul's grave and I made arrangements with a local priest to have it clearly marked, so that it could be easily moved to the British War Graves Cemetery in due course. I felt lonely. There was nothing left for me to do so I drove on to Kairouan, the eighth most holy city in the Mohammedan world. It was a fascinating ancient town. For centuries it had been held by the Moors; the souk was completely covered, built in the shape of a star. All the houses were white-washed, blank walls with huge nail-studded doors leading into pleasant shady courtyards. The mosque, with its pillars dragged from Carthage, was much as are all mosques with not a soul to be seen.

As I hurried back along the winding sandy track, I felt someone was following me. The town was dead silent and, sure enough, there was a naked man, scenting my track on all fours like a dog. I was thoroughly scared, for I was sure that he was a leper. I pounded on one of the huge doors and to my relief it opened. A most courteous, spotlessly attired elderly Arab invited me in. In perfect French, he offered me coffee, telling me that he was the head of the carpet making industry in the town. We chatted about Mecca to which he had made four pilgrimages, Cairo and Alexandria, both of which he knew well and of a priceless carpet Barbara Hutton had purchased recently. It was time for me to leave as I wanted to get back to the countryside before dark. As we made our adieux, he said, 'For the honour you have paid me, I will make a white carpet for you and it will remain here until you come again.' Thanking him, I doubted that I would ever pass that way again. 'You will,' he said, 'and you will find your carpet here.' I took Betty to Kairouan thirty years later; the old Arab was dead but his brother had my carpet, rolled and waiting for me.

Curiously enough, no-one enjoyed the peace of the sea-shore at Homs. We missed the daily excitement and the constant urge to get moving at all costs. With a day's notice we were told to do what we could to smarten our faded bush-jackets as the highest in the land was to inspect us. With red-hot sand in gin bottles we ironed them on the sea-shore, bleaching our belts and shoulder straps with salt water.

Then, setting out before dawn for an unknown destination, led by a military policeman, with my 3rd RHA on the right of the line, the whole division lined a road. Punctually at 10 a.m. down the road drove King George VI with General Montgomery. He stopped and shook hands with every commanding officer. A very proud moment!

I was ordered to return to the UK so, handing over 3rd RHA to Lt-Col Bill Norman, I drove to Algiers, where I found a huge headquarters preparing for the invasion of Sicily. With a large amount of tact and subtlety and assumed innocence, I managed to persuade a very high ranking American Air Force officer to provide me with a recommendation to be flown to the UK from Casablanca and, for good measure, a card of membership to the most exclusive club in Algiers, where I had been told the cocktails were out of this world. I

*Tunis
King George VI Reveiwing Units of the
7th Armoured Division
3rd Regiment Royal Horse Artillery*

wanted to fly home as I was far too scared to travel by ship. However I did send what kit I possessed back in some large ship I found in the Bay of Algiers.

The membership of the club I needed in order to give 'Cuba', one of Dudley Clarke's most attractive cypher girls whom I had known in Cairo, a pleasant evening – pleasant for me that is. Dudley was preparing the phoney landings for the benefit of the German troops in Sicily and very effective they proved to be. Personally I was completely uninterested except in my charming companion, who of course knew everyone. I flatly refused to join any high powered generals and, with difficulty, we managed to have a very good private dinner and an extremely pleasant evening. She fixed my flight next day to Marrakesh.

There I spent a few days as an honoured guest of the US Air Force. It is a delightful place, the garden of the French hotel had running water by the side of every path and the roses reputed to have been stolen from the Crusader prisoners of war were quite marvellous.

Chapter 14

INVASION PREPARATIONS

Looking back on the Western Desert campaign in which I had fought with Australians, Canadians, Poles, Free French, Americans, Maoris and many others, I thought of the many, many women scattered in far off places who mourned the loss of their men, husbands, lovers, sons, whom they would never see again, their resting places now marked by myriads of white crosses, planted in beautifully tended peaceful groves. I thought of that cruel, savage North African coast once more a testimony, as in the days of Rome and Carthage, of the futility of it all, now the radiance of the heroic deeds of so many brave men, faded into the brittle light of the African sun, so soon to be forgotten.

Safely home in Britain, I feigned complete idiocy, with the result a very pleasant ATS driver drove me from Prestwick to Pencraig. Here I found my mother and sister well, but nothing whatsoever remained of my warm barathea uniforms. All had been completely destroyed by moths, except for the gilt buttons. I was definitely not amused.

In due course I was given command of one of the best regiments I have ever come across. Privately I was told they were to be disbanded in a few weeks' time. I found them in Sussex, mostly sitting around in hundreds of holes in the ground, with Bren guns, ready to shoot at any marauding German fighters which happened to fly past. None had done so for the past two and a half years, so I changed all that and ordered all these mad keen youngsters a month of sport, fierce troop rivalry in which every officer and man had to participate. The result was astonishing.

London was so changed that I hardly knew it and I certainly did not care for it. I went to see Sinclair, now Director of Military Training, lamenting on the fate of this good regiment, but he could do nothing about it. However, he said I could take fifty of the officers, NCOs and men to whatever regiment I was eventually allotted.

Being so close to London suited me well. I retired to the Naval and Military Club every weekend. Mary Irwen, my bosom friend in our days in Cumberland, turned up frequently, garbed in the very smart uniform of a captain, charming curls and all. We had as happy a time as we could in that dreadfully overcrowded city. I found a nice flat for Betty near Harrods and soon she was home. For a month before it was disbanded the regiment was ordered to Kimberly Park in Norfolk, a large country house but totally unsuitable for housing 1,200 soldiers. The drains just gave up. I had some excellent days partridge driving with the tenant farmers whose families had all lived there for several generations. I also kept the officers' mess supplied with pheasants, much to the annoyance of the countess, who lived in a cottage nearby. The wife of one of the farmers supplied me with delicious home-made bread every few days. When we marched to church on Sunday 500 strong, the vicar was almost speechless. I exercised the various batteries in night operations. They were quite hopeless and invariably got lost; no-one had ever heard of navigating by the stars!

Very quickly the regiment disappeared and I betook myself with my chosen few to Yorkshire where I took command of a regiment of the Honourable Artillery Company; an excellent regiment it proved to be. As a very cold spring descended on Yorkshire, we were embroiled in manoeuvres with a Canadian armoured division. I was so cold I went to a large farm one night and begged shelter for the night. I said, 'I am dying of cold.'

'That's all right,' said the farmer's wife, 'you use the dining room; my father is also dying upstairs.' Too true, he died that night.

General Sinclair sought me out and asked how long I reckoned that the Canadian regiments with their Crusader tanks, armed with very light guns would last against the German Panther tanks. 'About twenty minutes a regiment or less,' I said. He was horrified. That was about right, for later on in Normandy I saw in front of me a squadron of Crusader tanks of the 44th Tank Regiment completely destroyed by two Panther tanks in about seven minutes. Everyone was burnt out.

One evening about 10 p.m., I was told to obtain a large field, cover it with heavy mesh wire netting, in which all the guns of the division could be assembled the next day, for inspection by the highest in the land, accompanied by his wife and two daughters.

Everyone worked flat out. One of my officers was sent to York to purchase a bottle of vintage port and one of Madeira. Betty took a lorry to the nearest large house, where she obtained with ease rugs, chairs, a table, hot water jugs and a large commode, all of which were installed in a small tent as a retiring room, for which she was most gratefully thanked. I found a small greenhouse nearby full of fabulous cyclamen, every plant had at least a hundred blooms. I bought the lot for £100 for the day, which the owner returned to me the following evening.

The king duly arrived on a fine but cold morning. He was most complimentary and the whole party retired to my beautifully decorated tent for coffee and every sort of hastily baked rolls. I may say all the local inhabitants knew of this visit long before I did!

Some high ranking officer thought that I should be promoted and posted to the 1st Airborne Division. I did not agree and said so, loud and clear. If, as was highly probable, I were to perish in the forthcoming campaign, I was determined to die on my feet with my many friends.

There was not much time to spare. I took all the guns up on to the wolds, giving all the young officers as much shooting practice as I could. I spent hours trying to prepare every man for what was to come. If they listened to me, certainly not more than half believed a word I said. They just could not imagine their opponents would be the highly efficient savage killers which I portrayed.

At last we all moved south with my regiment finishing up in the Horse Artillery Barracks in Aldershot, where the curtains that Betty had made for the men's dining hall windows some ten years before were still hanging. She rented a small but comfortable little house nearby where we spent our last few days together, with our two boxer dogs and a Siamese cat. Then it was up and away to whatever would come.

The crossing in a vast convoy of tank landing craft was both horrifying and perfectly peaceful. A nonchalant Texan commanded my small ship. He had done the trip before, we hadn't. The beaches were not particularly pleasant, with a certain amount of accurate shelling and the sad scattered remnant of the previous landing.

Following as quickly as possible the divisional signs, we moved fast inland, finally bivouacking in a quiet field. I put all the guns into action, just in case anything unforeseen should happen, which the men thought most tiresome.

Later that Sunday evening, I walked up to the tiny church of Cluny. I went in, sat down and promptly fell fast asleep. I awoke to find vespers in progress, with a white haired old curé, a few old village women in their picturesque Breton clothes and a man or two. 'Sleep on, young man,' he said, 'for you have far to go and so much to accomplish. We are honoured with your visit. Remember always our prayers will protect you.'

I was somewhat abashed but curiously comforted for I too had done all this before and indeed felt somewhat apprehensive of the future.

Chapter 15

THE CAMPAIGN IN FRANCE AND BELGIUM

I was now in command of the 13th Regiment Honourable Artillery Company of the Royal Horse Artillery in the 29th Armoured Brigade commanded by Brigadier Roscoe Harvey and part of the 11th Armoured Division commanded by Major General Roberts, yet again the spearhead in the advance of the army, this time across Europe,

We were fortunate to have arrived at all for, had the production of the two-men submarines, which I discovered months later at Surrendorf in Schleswig-Holstein, not been six months behind schedule, they would have caused havoc among the slow-moving tank landing craft, leaving most of our tanks at the bottom of the channel.

All my guns, mounted on Sherman tank chassis could, of course, accompany their respective tank regiments, wherever they went. They were to be in action continuously, by day and by night throughout the campaign. I could not speak more highly of this fine regiment, very well trained, staunch, brave and keen. My three battery commanders, Peter Gaunt, Bunny Davies and Bill Smith-Osborne, were of exceptionally high quality, especially Peter Gaunt, a man of great courage, always calm in moments of crisis, and an excellent gunner. He should have had a regiment of his own and he well deserved the DSO awarded to him at the end of the campaign. Sadly our casualties were to be very high, especially among the young forward observing officers (FOOs), hand-picked and highly efficient after interminable months of training in England. I, too, was fortunate in that all the regimental commanders in this brigade were personal friends of mine of many years standing. However, there was one individual, senior to me, whom we in Ireland were wont to call a 'Bog Irishman', who attempted to thwart me on certain occasions, mercifully without success.

It was now essential to break out of the beachhead, forcing back the encircling German armour. The 7th Armoured Division and the Guards Armoured Division were close by with the Americans away on the right flank. The first attempt made by the 7th Armoured Division was indecisive, the task proving more difficult than anticipated, due as much to the Normandy countryside as to the attentions of the scattered German armour. Plentifully

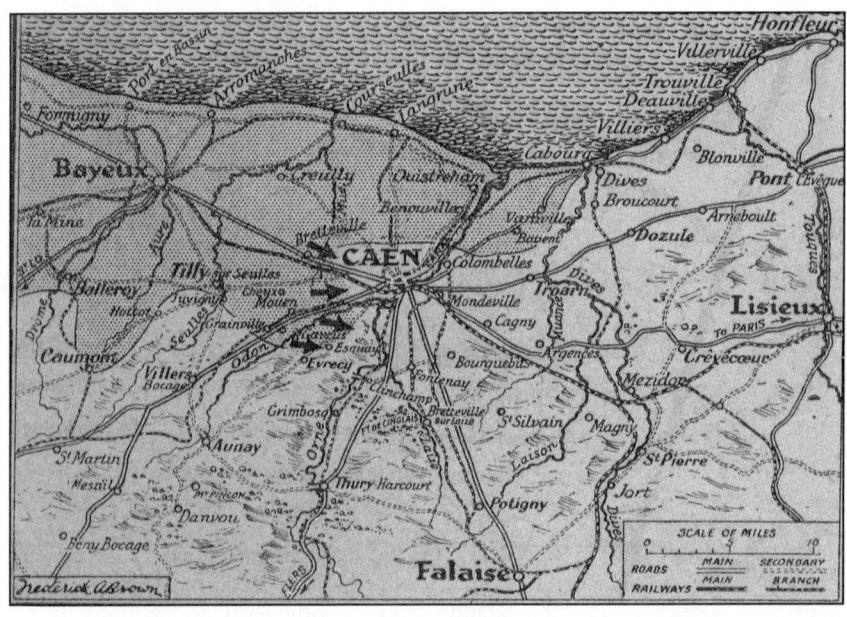

Colonel Bob's tank coming ashore in France

wooded with orchards and copses, the lanes, narrow, deep-set with thick impenetrable hedges, made our advancing tanks highly vulnerable.

It was now the turn of the 11th Armoured to attempt to break through. With our three tank regiments on the flanks, Roscoe and I, with a few HQ tanks, crossed the Odon stream early one morning, using an ancient brick bridge which shed a large number of bricks as each tank crossed over. All appeared peaceful the other side, a grassy field set with a small orchard. I tried out my machine gun on one of these plum trees and to my amazement, down jumped a couple of very young Germans, followed by a couple of very dead ones. With a few rounds into the remaining trees, we soon had 30 or 40.

They had left their rifles hanging in the branches, so they sat about looking miserable. I suppose they had been left there to discourage any of our infantry patrols and had speedily climbed up into the fruit trees on the sight of our tanks. There were Germans about all right, two Panther tanks opened up on us with solid shot; they were invisible in the woods quite close by. It was unpleasant but perhaps we were in a hollow for not a tank was hit. One of the Green Jacket patrols, moving up through the woods, called for artillery fire, so I deluged the woods with shells which discouraged the German infantry, if they were there, and forced the two Panther tanks to go elsewhere. The Germans then brought up some Minnenwurffer mortars and shelled us with their most unpleasant and noisy canisters, two of which bounced off my tank. I immediately called up a FOO with another tank, as it looked as if mine might shortly be put out of action. None of the tank regiments made much progress. One of our anti-tank regiments and the infantry brigade HQ removed themselves to the other side of the Odon. Nothing looked promising and I was not at all surprised when Roscoe told me that he had been instructed to withdraw about 10 p.m. when all the Green Jackets had passed through. Roscoe and his party set off, my tank wouldn't start, the battery was down. I was furious. Luckily my spare tank towed me out, though two tanks were almost too much for the old brick bridge.

General Montgomery now decided on launching a really heavy attack by all three armoured divisions, across the River Orne. There was only one narrow bridge left across the Orne, a large river which flowed through Caen. Should he achieve this, it would totally surprise the Germans, who did not for one moment consider this a feasible operation. Thus was initiated what became known as Operation Goodwood, now a much studied battle at our staff college.

Within a day we were on our way north to the Orne, where we lay up in thickets and orchards until dark. To get three armoured divisions across this one small bridge in one night was a daunting project. Nevertheless it was accomplished. Monty himself drove up and down the approach route to see that it was kept clear. Anything other than his armour found on the track was removed peremptorily.

Just before dawn the Pathfinders roared overhead dropping their flares which I had never seen before. A devastating attack by hundreds of planes of the Strategic

The Bocage

Air Force followed. Personally I saw very few dead Germans lying about after the raid, but no doubt some three or four thousand heavy bombs had a salutary effect on the countryside.

With great difficulty I brewed up a cup of tea, without which I cannot fight a battle, under a very smelly tarpaulin; not a light was allowed. We then set off, each tank following in the tracks of the one in front, as some enterprising sapper had strewn the place with mines and barbed wire, then wisely gone off to a quieter place.

Our objective was a small village called Quatre Bras on a hill about ten miles away. The two following armoured brigades were to deal with any Germans on the flanks. We were forbidden to do so, as the objective had to be achieved at all costs. My tank went slower and slower, finally stopping altogether. To my horror I found I was dragging about a mile of barbed wire and my sprocket wheels had eight feet of it tangled round them. There was nothing to be done except to cut through, taking it in turns with our only but very efficient wire cutters. This wasn't made any pleasanter by shells from the Lovat Scouts, firing from the other side of the Orne. I suppose their FOO had been killed. Anyway there was no means of telling them to stop shooting. All this took at least at least two hours and I was a long way behind Roscoe and his HQ. However, I found him at last sheltering under a steep railway embankment. Here he was being accurately shelled by devastating heavy German mortars. It was as unpleasant as it could be. Quite obviously there was a German FOO close by, for whenever we moved, the mortars followed. An RAF officer and his crew received two direct hits, killing them all; he was our link with the Typhoon bombers. Again I searched all round for this German FOO – then suddenly I got him. Except for brambles the embankment was bare, but in one place there was a large heap of pine branches. As there were no pine trees in the area, I immediately put a burst of machine gun fire into it and out staggered a badly wounded but brave young German officer with his signallers, all mortally wounded. He had done his best to kill us all and very nearly succeeded. We suffered no more from mortars.

Our tank regiments had been suffering severe losses all along the noisy, dusty advance, mostly from two Panther tanks hidden in a thick hedge on our left flank. They have since claimed about a hundred of our tanks were knocked out. They may well be right but personally I did not see any burning so most were probably recoverable, though with depleted crews. Towards evening, Roscoe, having captured our objective – the village of Quatre Bras – after a desperate hand-to-hand fight, handed over to the 7th Armoured Division, who had at last arrived, hours late. They and the Guards Armoured Division continued the advance, forcing the German armour back to the Falaise Gap. Tragically the Americans arrived too late to close the trap completely. Nevertheless the breakout was accomplished but at what a horrible cost in well trained tank crews. I had a blinding headache, chiefly due to not having had time to get a meal of any sort during the day, accompanied by the appalling noise and acute danger.

The rain now come down in torrents. I pulled back into what had been a large farm, now a heap of rubble. As night drew on some pet Belgian hares came back looking for their hutches. I picked up two beautiful grey ones and they remained with me throughout the campaign, having numerous families in awkward places. During the night the pitiful remains of our brigade made their way back across the Orne. I can't remember anything at all of this. I think that, for the only time in my life, I had passed out with sheer fatigue.

Within a couple of days, most of the tanks had been repaired, new ones brought up and the gaps in the crews made up to strength. The advance set off again, this time the division passed east of Caen and soon we were forging ahead through the beautiful Bocage country of Normandy.

Early one morning in the station yard of the small village of Flers, a train of cattle trucks was assembling for Dachau. It was filled with Jews of all stations of life, who would never return. Suddenly our leading tanks appeared; we had won through after a particularly fierce engagement with the remnants of a German tank division. All the Germans in the station ran away and the Jews thankfully jumped out of the cattle trucks to go home to their breakfast. The inhabitants of the village have never forgotten this morning. They put up a very simple but fine memorial to our 1,200 dead and some thirty years later invited members of the 11th Armoured Division to visit, giving them a fantastic reception. Some 500-600 officers and men with their wives were entertained for three days.

Now it was on to Paris at top speed. I crossed the Seine at Vernon on an extremely unsafe bridge of boats, certainly never intended to carry tanks. It was pitch dark, dead quiet, not a soul about. I could not find Roscoe although I knew he had crossed just in front of me. Extraordinary how alone you feel when everything is dead quiet, so I pulled back to the bridge and waited there until the dawn came, then I found Roscoe with a few of the tanks of the 23rd Hussars, only a few hundred yards away. We all had a good breakfast, plenty of eggs in France, before moving on again. Of course I didn't know that the entry into Paris was reserved for General de Gaulle, quite rightly, so it was disappointing as we passed a signpost – Paris 10 kilometres – to receive express orders to by-pass the city and press on at all speed. Savage fighting just flared up totally unexpectedly in a matter of minutes. I was watching a column of five to six hundred German prisoners, carrying no weapons, marching along the road, when half a dozen Panther tanks appeared out of some gorse bushes, in front of me, firing blindly. Peter Gaunt's battery was up with us. The German prisoners en masse just went for the guns. They did no damage before disappearing again over the hill, but left a lot of dead behind; it certainly was a free for all. I had four or five jump on the back of my tank. I fancy they all fell off. They were brave men. I expect they knew where they were, which we did not.

That evening at dusk a French farmer, driving home his cows, told me that a large number of Germans had collected in a small village ahead, where they were obviously going to spend the night. I believed him, Roscoe did not. However he agreed to let me open up on the village with all the guns I could get just after dark. We gave them ten rounds per gun from three regiments. Next morning I went along to see the result. It was appalling, dead Germans everywhere, all their lovely horses killed still harnessed to the wagons. The village appeared unscathed. In the tiny square a long trestle table was laid with a meal and wine for some forty officers which they had had no time to eat. There was not a soul about except a large number of bemused wounded. All very pathetic, but so is war.

We drove on all through that night – it was pitch dark. Each tank followed the tiny red rear light of the one in front, the column never stopped and there were no halts. Just before dawn, we were conscious of a large number of vehicles and armour, crowding the roads and tracks alongside us. Unwittingly we had cut through one of the German main lines of retreat. There was considerable confusion; my staff car followed the wrong line of tanks for a couple of hours before realising the mistake. Wisely they took to the fields, even so I was very lucky ever to see them again. My driver, a doleful Welshman from Swansea, did not recover for several days, never letting my tank out of his sight!

With the dawn, we found ourselves very close to Amiens, we had indeed come a long way. There were a lot of dejected-looking German infantry men wandering about. We could not be bothered with them and that made them even more miserable. I was too tired to sleep, so I borrowed Roscoe's jeep, driving up to a small farm at the top of the hill, where I found a couple of platoons of the Rifle Brigade, dead asleep in the straw of the barn. I woke the young officer up and we walked up to the door of the farm, kicking it open. I was amazed to see a German general with a couple of his officers, sitting down to breakfast. I was very annoyed, I suppose because I was very hungry. I told them to finish their meal, for they certainly would not get another that day. With considerable reluctance the young, very good-looking staff officer gave me his Luger which I was delighted to have. The general seemed unconcerned. He surrendered his papers quite willingly. Among them I found a most interesting document. It was a postcard, unsigned, addressed to the general, depicting a German regular soldier holding his head in his arm, blood dripping down. I kept it though no-one would tell me what it signified. A year later I was told that it was the method used to warn all the generals that the bomb attack on Hitler had failed to kill him and that the German regular army was doomed. I have it here in my war book. I doubt that another is in existence.

On and on, we never seemed to stop. How the tanks stood it, I can't think but they were well made, with excellent engines. Talk about our advance across the desert from Alamein, that was a crawl compared with this. Thank goodness we were to halt for a day, while someone made up their mind whether to drop the 1st Airborne Division in front of us. A waste of time for I did not think there were any large forces of Germans in this area. We couldn't be far from Brussels now, I did hope we would be allowed to liberate that lovely city! Not a hope, we were to by-pass it again and make sure of Antwerp, leaving Brussels to the Guards Armoured Division.

My two Belgian hares which had accompanied me from Caen had just produced eight babies. They lived on army biscuits in a box in my staff car, quite a problem. I should have left it to my Driver Jones.

The German commanding officer in Brussels asked that it should be declared an open city, in return he would evacuate it with every German soldier under his command, without a shot being fired. This was agreed, so Roscoe and I drove in for lunch to have a look-round and see how things were going. He wanted to look up an old friend called Henri le Grand but we could not find his house.

A most delightful-looking woman walking up the street was the only person in sight, so we stopped her. She jumped in, saying she knew Roscoe's friend well; he was not at home. Roscoe went off somewhere while she and I walked back to her flat for tea. She offered me a hot bath, which I suddenly realised was much needed. She took me, much refreshed, to a large and wildly excited cocktail party.

The Guards Armoured Division was due to make its ceremonial entry the following day, so Roscoe and I were the unheralded liberators and did they welcome us! I was charmed beyond words with my companion, Madame Renée Depage. Later we dined in a large restaurant at the Rond Point, again crowded with her friends. I ate a good dinner, the best I had had for many a day but I don't think many others did. Frantic cheering and chanting greeted every new arrival. Fortunately Roscoe turned up, else I should never have seen my regiment again. From this chance encounter, a firm friendship developed between Renée and myself, which lasted until her death twenty years later.

Away again at dawn, we were soon approaching Antwerp, a comparatively peaceful journey. Frequently, young men of the Resistance appeared from nowhere. They were most useful, telling us of bridges blown or defended, and guiding us across country, where men who were ploughing dropped everything, running across the fields to salute us. In the villages as we passed, they dealt savagely with the girls who had collaborated with the Germans, shaving their heads, then throwing them over the bridge into the local river. When we met up with any German pocket of resistance, they lay on the back of the tanks, leaping off to administer any coup-de-grâce necessary and they would then go off into the woods to round up a few more Germans and take their rifles and ammunition. This was a great saving in time for us and most useful.

Chapter 16

THE CAPTURE OF ANTWERP
AND ON INTO HOLLAND AND GERMANY

Antwerp, our goal, was in sight. Every man in the Armoured Brigade was covered in dust and tired beyond words. The speed of this advance was without comprehension, an average of 53 miles per day. The main bridge had been blown, but the men of the Resistance led us along a small side road and over a very flimsy wooden bridge, nevertheless it carried us over. The German garrison of the city had no idea of our arrival; 3,000 men surrendered without a shot, but not the garrisons of the forts and block-houses, mostly the other side of the Schelde, which gave us a great deal of trouble. All the tanks disappeared in a moment through the city, making for the docks.

Brigadier Roscoe Harvey

The whole city exploded, a mass of cheering people thronged every open space, as the tanks passed, girls and Resistance men stepped off the balconies with bottles of champagne, hanging on somehow when the shells and mortars fell.

Roscoe and I were in a large square simply solid with people when down came a few shells and mortars. Fortunately there appeared few casualties; two girls and a young man received an almost direct hit by a mortar on the front of my tank. They were killed outright. I was so mad I pulled off into a side-street, rows of terraced houses. I stopped opposite one of them, the door opened immediately and a charming elderly man in very correct attire invited me to come upstairs. Telling my crew to 'brew up', I followed him up a very narrow staircase. This opened into a large room, rather like the dining room of White's Club in St James. Two chefs presided over a long table of every imaginable cold dish, champagne was flowing, while about fifty of the city's most influential men welcomed me. To say I was rendered speechless, would be an understatement. I was filthy. I could hardly see out of my dust-covered eyes. Not one of the exquisitely dressed men took any notice at all. They just sat me down and gave me a superb lunch. They gathered round and said, 'Mon Colonel, you do not know it, but you are superb, you are the most welcome visitor this club has entertained for several years. Is there anything we can do for you?'

I said, 'Yes, will anyone cash me a cheque for £5. I want to purchase some silk stockings for my wife.'

A grey-haired elderly man stepped forward, saying, 'Sir, it is my pleasure.' He took my cheque and gave me a handful of Belgian notes. I thanked them all and took my leave. A young man followed me down saying, 'I will help you buy the silk stockings.'

We both climbed into my tank. As we crawled along, he said, 'That man who cashed your cheque for £5 is the chairman of the largest bank in Antwerp, the richest city in Europe. That cheque of yours is already worth thousands of pounds, proof positive of what every soul in this city has yearned for - "Liberation", signed and sealed by you.' He took me to a small boutique, closed and barred. Calling lustily he brought down from the flat above a most attractive girl, whom he obviously knew very well. She quickly produced a dozen pairs of lovely silk stockings for Betty. We both kissed her good-bye and went our respective ways.

The day wore on with sniping and occasional shelling. Roscoe sent me a young man who said some Germans were holding out in a blockhouse nearby and would I deal with it. I got hold of Buck Taylor, one of my most efficient young officers; he had risen from the ranks and had already won a good MC in Normandy. I told him to take one of the 25-pounders and put ten rounds into the blockhouse; on no account was he to approach it, until it was completely demolished. For some unknown reason, he did not do this but drove up to the house in his half-track vehicle. Here he was met by heavy machine gun fire;

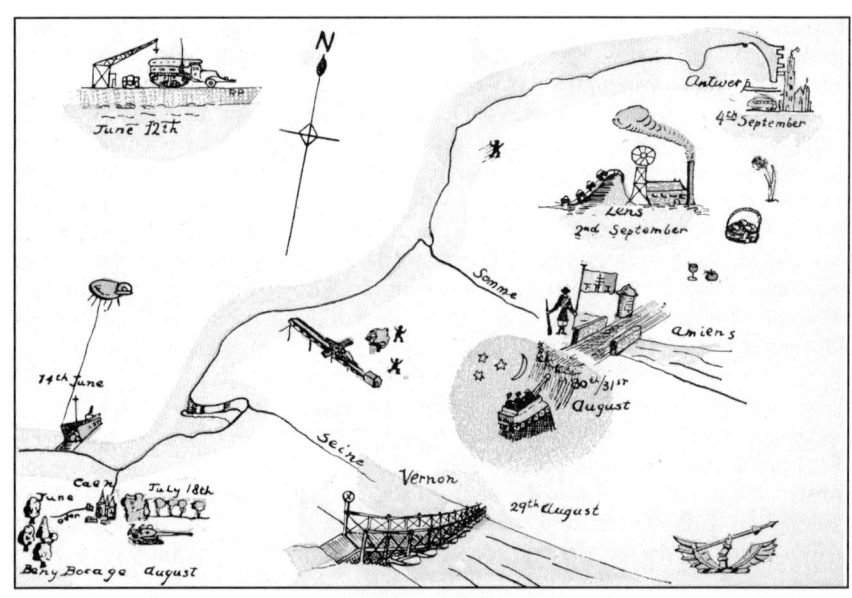

Sketch map of France and Belgium, 1944

Antwerp

four of his men were killed and he and one other badly wounded. When I heard about this, I was simply furious and went there myself. The Germans had gone; I found Taylor unconscious lying on a kitchen table, his wounded companion was dead. Oh, what a waste of good men. Later that evening, when Taylor was in an ambulance full of wounded, the driver in the dusk mistook the bridge and drove straight into the canal, with water sixteen feet deep. Taylor managed to get out and swam to the bank four times dragging a man with him. He then passed out. A couple of civilians carried him to a small convent nearby. I heard nothing of this for a couple of days. When I went to see him, the mother superior said he was dying. All he wanted was a loaf of white bread but there was no white bread in Antwerp. It was about ten o'clock at night and I set off to find the nearest American unit. I found them and they gave me some white loaves, which I left at the convent about dawn. Taylor recovered completely and is alive today. I got him a decoration for his bravery.

Just before Roscoe and I pulled out of the city that first evening, I had to circumvent a mass of burning furniture in the middle of the street, it was being thrown out of the windows of a large house, which belonged to a collaborator who had committed frightful atrocities on elderly people, so I was told. As I shrewdly suspected that the occupants of the house would soon follow their furniture, I drove on. Roscoe spent the night in a charming chateau, surrounded by a moat, where he could sleep in peace. I went to a large house next door. The comte and comtesse were in bed but their 17-year old daughter welcomed me. In no time she had an excellent dinner prepared for me and two large buckets of hot soup for my tank crew and others who were with me. I just slept on the floor where I had dined.

During the night, small parties of the more audacious Germans crossed the Schelde, shooting at anyone they saw. As ill luck would have it, some of them came across a young intelligence officer of mine and four of his men walking round the garden after breakfast the next morning. They shot them all among the roses in the garden. I was caught walking over to Roscoe's castle but luckily the tennis courts had been planted up with cabbages, so for half an hour I had to crawl about, getting more and more dirty and more and more infuriated. At last one of Roscoe's tank crews awoke to what was happening and opened fire on the bushes all round and that finished it. When I got back I found the comte and comtesse speechless with horror at what had occurred in the rose garden. They just could not believe it. Their daughter fetched the gardeners, so we buried my men where they fell; she assured me that she would tend the graves until members of the War Graves Commission arrived. She was a brave 17-year old.

The tragedy of the whole operation was that, for some reason, General Roberts did not insist on our lorried infantry brigade infiltrating through the actual docks, which we of course could not do. The result was that the Germans quickly made strong defences on the far side so that we could not use the docks for another three weary months. Within a very few days, Monty, who was very conscious of the frailty of our long thin line of communication, ordered the whole division to move eastwards into Holland to safeguard against this threat. A wise precaution but not at all a popular one with us. The following is an extract from the Antwerp local newspaper, Het Handelsblad van Antwerpen, dated 14th September, 1944 :

> Never will Antwerp be able to express in full its gratitude to the heroes of the 11th British Armoured Division. Through their unmatched courage and the speed of their heavy tanks they overcame every difficulty and broke down all resistance.
>
> People of Antwerp: it was with a noise like thunder that these long unending columns of steel monsters roared their way from Normandy to the north. For Antwerp was their goal – that city which by virtue of its situation on the east bank of the River Schelde had become the sole way of escape for the German troops in north-east France and Flanders. This escape route had to be cut, and cut it was by the unexpected speed and outstanding daring of the advance by night as well as by day – 700 kilometres in nine days,
>
> Who could have expected it, when under conditions of utmost secrecy and great danger we listened to the BBC and learnt that the British had crossed the Seine and reached Beauvais by way of Gisors. The slow advance in Normandy had not prepared us for the lightning-like thrusts which were to follow. The first surprise came with the announcement of the capture of Amiens.
>
> Such were the conditions which gave rise to the following incident. At Beauvais it was decided, as the supply of petrol was just sufficient, to push on to Amiens. Night was already falling and the troops tired after a day's fighting through unknown country and over roads rendered even more difficult to see by driving rain. The tanks roared their way through the night with a muted noise like thunder. Incidents arose now and then as this column cut across the main retreat of the Germans. British tanks and German tanks got mixed up together but they sorted themselves out. The advance never stopped and there were no serious hold-ups.
>
> Just before Amiens was reached the main bridge over the Somme was blown, but the soldiers of the FFI had succeeded in capturing three other bridges and the advance was not halted. No time was lost in Amiens and, after a brief rest, the advance went on. On! On! Always on!
>
> During the night of the Saturday/Sunday, the Belgian frontier was crossed. Towns which might have resisted were by-passed and left to the formations following up behind.
>
> I remember when on Sunday I was watching the Germans escaping through the tunnel, I was thought mad to suggest that this very day would see Brussels free and that the city of Antwerp would be liberated on the following day. Even I hesitated to express this opinion, though I knew it was only a matter of a few days.

But even while we stood there, already in the distance the columns of the irresistible British Armoured Division were approaching. When I was told on Monday morning, 'They are in Malines and Boom,' I could hardly believe my ears and yet it was true.

The broad river Rupel was crossed without any obstacle, thanks to the outstanding courage of a civilian whose name has been given to me. This man extinguished the burning fuse and the bridge was saved. By eleven o'clock the tanks were already in front of the defences of Antwerp. The remainder of the story is already known.

The shouts of joy, the scenes of wild enthusiasm – these will never be forgotten and served as first proof of our gratitude to the heroes of the 11th Armoured Division who, covered in dust and half dead with fatigue, brought us the liberation which had been so long awaited and was yet entirely unexpected.

Now we made a slow advance into Holland. The lines of communications were stretched to the limit, so we had to await the Americans and some consolidation. Then it was Arnhem, a tragic affair; we were there on the other side of the river but they could not contact my guns, nor could the tanks of the Guards Armoured Division force the bridge. Such a lot of fine men were killed. I wonder that it was ever considered as a feasible operation. Hereabouts there were a few pockets of well dug in German paratroopers who fought bravely, only to die in the end.

About mid-day one morning we passed a massive castle surrounded by a moat. It certainly held Germans and appeared to be on fire at the rear when, out of a grating just above the water level, appeared a woman's arm waving. Several men waded over but could not understand a word of her French. In the end, I very reluctantly removed my trousers and boots and waded over. She looked most attractive and explained that there was a small postern further round; if we could blow it in, she could then get out. All went to plan; there were two of us now in my tank wrapped in blankets. The Germans surrendered and were made to put out the fire.

On we crawled. I had a fine heavy machine gun, which I had captured and had just fixed to my tank. I was longing to use it, when a couple of German officers drove furiously towards us up a narrow side-road. My gun proved most effective, blowing the front of the car to smithereens. The officers ran off, as the gun jammed. When I reached the car, I opened a small suitcase to find it packed with new French notes. At that moment, I was called to the wireless by one of my FOOs who was in trouble so I told a young subaltern who was on my tank to jump down and fetch the suitcase. He was too interested helping the woman we had rescued to dry her hair. He waited too long and was forestalled by an officer of the 23rd Hussars, who was just behind us. None of the 23rd Hussars ever let a good thing go by. He got the suitcase and all that cash, which allowed all their officers free champagne for the remainder of the campaign. I cursed them all, the girl included. She had a hunting lodge a mile or two further on, where she invited me to dinner, saying I could shoot as many of her pheasants as I pleased. A few days later, I did just this. I intended billeting myself on her for as long as we were in the vicinity, when, to my fury, I found myself again forestalled, this time by a great friend of mine, who commanded a regiment that I had not seen for weeks and I was certain he was nowhere about. He was firmly ensconced in an armchair in front of the fire, in his carpet slippers!

It then rained every day for two weeks, becoming very cold. I was in a small farm, very smelly – lots of cows, not at all on a par with that hunting lodge. However, the farmer's wife had a magnificent array of enormous round cheeses. I bought the lot – and even sent one back to Betty in England, as 'a gift from a British soldier'. It reached her intact in Suffolk, where she had just purchased a lovely old house, destined to be our happy home for many years to come. The rain never stopped; the closer we got to the River Maas the more awful the mud until, like every army throughout the ages which had endeavoured to campaign in the Low Countries in the winter, we became bogged down and completely static wherever we happened to be.

With several pheasants, a chicken and two huge cheeses, I drove back to Brussels to stay with Renée Depage, where I washed off the mud, leading a very pleasant civilised life with my charming companion for forty-eight hours.

Christmas 1944 came; I gave each battery an enormous pig and everyone had an excellent Christmas dinner, though our living conditions in the cowsheds were dreadful. There was nowhere else to go as it was a very poor part of Holland. Early on new year's morning, I was up in a church tower where, to my amazement, I saw what seemed like a hundred and more German fighter planes hedge-hopping below me. I got through to our corps headquarters warning them of these planes bound for Brussels aerodrome I was sure. No one believed me and they did a great deal of damage, destroying many of our densely packed aeroplanes, but only a few got back over the Maas.

General Bolo Whistler, whom I had known in the desert, arrived and took over our defensive role with elements of his division, while we pulled back on to higher ground, where at least there were a few houses to shelter in. We tried to think it was nicer, but it wasn't – colder in fact. Away to the north of us, heavy fighting was taking place. I drove up there in a jeep to see what was going on. It was so awful – an infantry fight in the Hochenfeld Forest – British and German dead everywhere lying in heaps, smashed houses, smashed vehicles and mud feet deep. So bad that I turned round fast and made for home.

General Rundstedt had had his offensive through the Ardennes. He and his armour gave everyone a nasty shock until all his tanks and lorries ran out of petrol. The Americans put up a great fight at Bastogne. Roscoe was ordered down there with every tank he could muster, but he was not needed; neither was I or my guns.

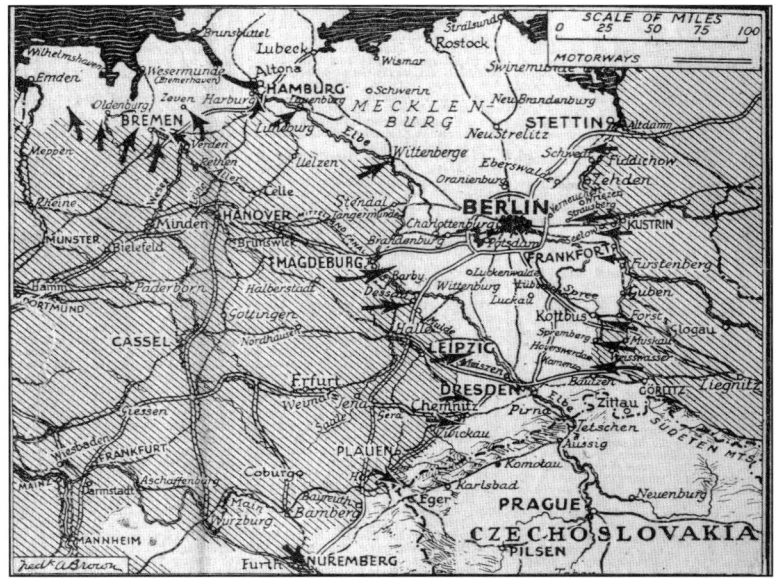

We were not far from the Rhine at that point and we thought we would soon be crossing it. There were no German planes but lots of V2 were going up in the distance. A lot of gliders came down on both sides of the Rhine. Our bridge of boats was nearly complete; it floated, it rocked but it held. We would soon all be across. Curiously enough the Germans had not disputed the crossing at Wessel at all, though there were plenty of them about somewhere. There certainly were a couple of miles from the Rhine. We passed four gliders, packed with men, apparently safely landed in a couple of fields. When I got up to them, I found each one burnt out and all the occupants were dead. For some tragic reason they had mistaken their way and had landed almost on top of a well dug in and well camouflaged position holding six 88mm guns. Why those deadly guns were there I couldn't imagine. A platoon of the Rifle Brigade accompanying us got mixed up with these German gun crews. They were heavily outnumbered and Bill Budgeon, one of the very best of my young officers, went to their aid. He was shot dead but his tank crew managed to extricate what was left of the platoon. His battery commander, Major Peter Gaunt, brought his body up to me in the afternoon; he was in tears and Peter certainly was a tough soldier. We buried Bill there and then, while at least a company of the Rifle Brigade arrived to pay their respects to a most gallant officer, whom they held in very high esteem.

All the armour was halted alongside a deep canal, where there was a passable bridge. On the other side of the canal the ground sloped up sharply, cutting off all forward vision. All the afternoon a single 88mm had been firing one shot up into the sky every few minutes; otherwise there was an eerie silence. I did not like it, I felt something was very wrong. I had never known any German gun crew give away its position so blatantly. General Roberts arrived; Roscoe wanted to get as much of the armour as possible across the bridge before dark. General Roberts did not want to allow the armour to become separated, nor did he like the look of the bridge. He asked me what I thought. I told him that I thought there was something wrong and sinister about the place. So they compromised and decided to send a battalion, which had just joined us straight out from England, to cross over and make a firm bridgehead before dark. The battalion took a long time to arrive. Just before dark, they crossed over and we could see them digging in on the slope nearest to us and their fires cooking their evening meal. Suddenly without any warning, down from the top of the slope came a couple of hundred Germans with fixed bayonets. The whole attack was over in ten minutes, the Germans disappeared, leaving 60% of that battalion dead or dying in front of us. We were powerless to help them. We poured shells over the ridge in the darkness but I doubt if they damaged anybody. A very sad and untidy affair.

We crossed over next morning and there beyond the hill was a battle training camp for NCOs. Not a soul was to be seen. In their training they must have often practised this operation which was so successful. One can mourn and grieve for the dead but in war one has to go on all the time. We were to come across another battle school very shortly; fortunately the casualties on that occasion were on the enemy side,

Next morning Roscoe went off in his jeep to meet David Silvertop and one of the COs of a lorried infantry battalion at an arranged cross-roads. Within minutes two German half-track vehicles came round the corner at speed; the first one drove straight into a wall and overturned, the second one opened fire at once on Roscoe's small party standing under the hedge. David Silvertop, an infantry CO and another man were killed outright; Roscoe escaped with a slight flesh wound. On it drove, fortunately straight into one of our tanks, where it was immediately destroyed. The damage was done.

The weather had vastly improved and so it should as it was now April. We would soon be in that wonderful farmland, the Rhineland. Now that we were in Germany, I never slept rough. About dusk, I would choose a nice-looking farm, ordering everyone out in about twenty minutes; having looked round for 'lurkers', I would spend a most comfortable warm night. Very naturally, there were small parties of German troops all over the place, especially Hitler Youth, who were most troublesome. They lay in the ditches with bazookas, feigning death, blowing off the tracks on tanks as they passed by. I found a grenade the best deterrent. At this time we had a fierce engagement at a river crossing with some paratroopers – definitely a nasty lot. Once I took refuge in a small black barn where to my delight I found a dump of certainly six hundred bottles of excellent white wine, which partially made up for a most dangerous couple of days. We had to wait for a day or two while the divisions came up on either side of us, prior to crossing the Elbe. The farm I had chosen had the most beautiful horses, cattle and pigs, all run by Russian slave labour. At each end of the charming farmhouse was a small wooden platform where two pairs of storks had built their nests. I had never seen this before and was fascinated. While we were lying on the lawn, drinking our white wine, a pair of most elegant silk-clad legs appeared in front of me. I really could not be bothered with her, but her story was interesting. Apparently she was the mistress of one of the high-ranking Nazis, who had fled to Sweden. She and her child and nurse were sent to this farm household, who were ordered to care for her and feed all three. She was not enthusiastic about their care and thought maybe I could be persuaded to take her on. I told her to go away, as I could not care less whether she lived or died: Floods of tears! She certainly was a beauty, so my intelligence officer kept telling me.

I put quite a lot of heavy shells into a large town the other side of the Elbe; this thoroughly frightened everyone. White flags appeared in every house and no-one even shot at us as we crossed the river. As we went through some large forest, the foresters were most troublesome. They were excellent shots. Dressed in Austrian green, they stood like ramrods in front of fir trees and were quite invisible. I know I killed at least one; I never even saw all the others.

The country east of the river stretched away in front of us; every lane had hedges of flowering lilac. The German resistance, though savage at times, was definitely lessening. Roscoe and I with half a dozen tanks went by chance into a small village, where I saw a tall very good-looking Panzer grenadier walk into the little square. He fired a red verey light and immediately every soul in that village fought ferociously. The two men in the tank in front of me were shot dead by an eleven year old, from a first floor window. The doors of the small houses opened and out came a plank, followed by a barrel of flaming oil. Hordes of very young Hitler Youth ran all over the place, throwing grenades. It was another battle training camp for the 17-year olds. We pulled back and then I shelled it; that was the end for the Hitler Youth. When I was walking round the village, I saw a badly wounded boy lying on the doorstep of a house. No-one came to his help, so I shot the lock away, ordered everyone out of the house and told them to carry the boy in and attend to his wounds. They were callous beyond words, those Germans. The Panzer grenadier was lying in a small garden; he was dying and, by his head, sat the most beautiful Titian red silky long-haired Dachshund I had ever seen. I called to him, he followed me and lived in my tank for the next few days and then with the Belgian hares in my staff car. We became devoted to each other; he returned to England with me and settled down in Suffolk until he died.

On 18th April we ran into a party of five hundred prisoners of war. They were all sick and had to fall out of their columns the day before. I chatted to them. All the worst cases were lying in a barn with a British medical officer looking after them. All that could walk swarmed over the tank, getting food and cigarettes. They were terribly quiet and some just could not speak. I turned every German out of the farmhouse, so at least they could be comfortable until transport arrived to take them back. I found a sergeant of the 2nd RHA and he told me a lot of 3rd RHA and 4 RHA passed through last night. Those blasted Germans – just for spite they had marched thousands across the Elbe away from us. All these men had been prisoners since 1940 so you can just imagine what this day meant to them.

The day before we had had a very tough fight. When we took the place in the evening, the inhabitants calmly came out of their cellars and were much annoyed when our men would not help them put out the fires in the blazing houses. Every house that harboured snipers was dealt with like that. Excellent thing!

From the top of the hill, one could see miles of rolling farmland. There were columns of dust coming from the east. As the columns approached us, we could see that they consisted of farm wagons filled with corn sacks and the families riding their ponies or horses alongside. The grandmother and grandfather sat at the back. When they died, they were just lifted down and left on the side of the road. All these hundreds of people were fleeing from the Russians. Whether they had seen the Russians or not, I don't think the Russians had a very good reputation.

A very large, fat and untidy-looking German officer, with no hat and coat all open, came running down the road, waving his arms, shouting, 'There is typhus ahead, at all costs you must not go on.' We paid no attention to him whatever and we came to a group of buildings with an archway of laurels and a guard with gilt buttons and a little officer with a gilt sword. They were Romanians. This was a political concentration camp at a place called Belsen. Here they went in for slow starvation. There were thousands of men and women too weak to get even their ration of half a litre of soup from the cook-houses. Three thousand unburied corpses were lying about in the compounds. A hospital had no blankets and no medical equipment. Four-tier beds with three emaciated people in each bed, some with diseases and others with bullet wounds from the SS guards, waiting to die. They died as you watched them, 800 deaths a day. I saw the open trucks they had been brought in during winter with desiccated corpses still lying in them. These things were unbelievable but true.

I saw the gas ovens. As they had run out of fuel, they could not burn the bodies. They were packed into an enormous trench, thousands of them. We were not fighting human beings at all, but evil incarnate, such as the world had never seen and I am sure will forget only too soon. I passed the notorious Irma Grece, the terror of Belsen prisoners, with her alsatian; she gave one look at me and disappeared. The guards were Waffen SS. Some while ago the BBC was going to allow one of the officers of the Waffen SS to go over to England and persuade us that the Waffen SS were not the horrors that they in fact were. I

British prisoners liberated by R.B.T Daniell

Batch of German prisoners

wrote to the BBC when I heard of this and told them what I had seen at Belsen. I received a very civil letter in reply and this officer of the Waffen SS was stopped from lecturing in this country.

Round the sheds where people were lying in straw, there was a large number of men and women impaled on the barbed wire waiting to die; they had mostly been shot in the back. They had heard the noise of the guns and they couldn't wait any longer. They tried once more to get out of this absolute hell, but not one of them lived. I am a marksman but a very bad shot with a revolver and that day I was very sorry of that fact, for very few of the SS guards whom I shot at did I kill. A pity!

When I opened the first long hut, at the door was lying a dead, completely naked woman and on her body were sitting five or six small children, playing that game when you have different lengths of straw. It was too horrifying for words. It started off in quite a small way as a camp of 900 political prisoners, then they sent a thousand, then two thousand, then goodness knows how many thousand regularly and there was no more food than there was originally for the 900, with a result that they were just waiting to die of slow starvation, which is indeed a terrible death.

Roscoe, wisely, didn't come in but he sent Charles Chapman, who commanded a light ack-ack battery and told him to do what he could until they could get up a medical team from corps headquarters to deal with this appalling place. I have told people, in the years since then, some of the things that I saw at Belsen and I don't honestly think more than one in ten believed me. Memories are very short but it is up to us who have seen these things to try and persuade other people that they must never, never happen again.

I went back two days later with General Roberts and Roscoe and we went to see how Charles Chapman was getting on and whether the medical teams had arrived, which indeed they had. I was pleased to see Irma Grece, who had used her alsatian to tear these people to pieces, standing in the middle of this ditch. She had no clothes on whatsoever and she bad been told to go through the bodies to see if any of them were still alive. Their practice was, if anyone survived the ill-treatment, to throw them in the ditch alive and leave them there to die. Every corpse in the ditch, and there must have been two or three thousand, was completely naked. It was a horrifying spectacle.

For two or three days now we had paid little or no attention to the Germans because we had been racing the Russians to the Baltic so as to stop them going through into Denmark and Sweden. We had gone on without stopping and at last we reached the Baltic, at Lübeck. Cairo to the Baltic – it was unbelievable, but it was a fact. Lübeck itself is a charming town, and was totally untouched by the war; all the roads were lined with apple trees in full blossom. It was a lovely place with several very large hospitals.

Roscoe asked me to take charge of a barracks where he was told there were a thousand and more police and SS who wanted to surrender. I went up there in a jeep with my driver. The police did not want a fight at all but I did not like the look of the four hundred SS, so I sent for my tank. Then I stood on that and ordered all arms and revolvers to be piled in the centre of the square. The commandant was most helpful and it all went off without a murmur. We did feel a little naked, just the two of us, especially when some German planes roared over head and dropped some bombs some way away and, by ill chance, killed four of my men. It was pitch dark by the time I had handed the police camp over to an anti-tank battery and midnight before I got some dinner. I then went into the nearest house, rolled into a most comfortable warm bed and slept like a top.

One day I passed a lot of horses, there must have been two or three hundred of them, led by a Uhlan woman – a German, she had a lot of Polish and German girls with her looking after them. She said she had brought them up from Munster. It seemed that they had something to do with the Aga Khan's stud wherever that was, but they were of more interest to Roscoe than they were to me.

It was rather like the end of the desert campaign. German generals, officers of all sorts, Luftwaffe girls, SS dressed in slave labourers' clothes – all wanted to be taken prisoner. Then they thought they would be safe. They were definitely very frightened people. I fear the really guilty ones were all slipping away.

UNCONDITIONAL SURRENDER OF ALL GERMAN FORCES

THE 1939 - 1945 WAR IS OVER

Drumhead Service -

Sunday, 16th May, 1943 at Tunis.
Sunday, 6th May, 1945 at Lübeck.

Roscoe Harvey and I were together and what a war we had fought. It was hardly credible that we had never been touched. The fine regiment of gunners, the 13th HAC, RHA had fought magnificently, excellently led by their battery commanders and superbly served by all their young officers; never were they slow to answer a call for the guns, though at times too tired to think.

I had led them a long way through most bitter fighting with a savage and unpredictable enemy. In spite of all my care of them, the hazards had been too great at times. I mourned the deaths of so many brave men who would never recross the Channel with me.

From the first time that I met General Montgomery, I liked him. He was a true soldiers' commander; he never minced words, he had no use for the second rate. He meant what he said. It must never be forgotten that he took over a beaten and tired remnant of what had been a proud and well trained force, imbuing them once more, in a pitiably few weeks, into the tough fighting force they had once been.

Of his human side, so little is known. A few weeks before the unleashing of the greatest army the world has ever known into a thoroughly hazardous operation, he took the trouble to come down and listen to my problems, those of a very junior but experienced commanding officer. He sat beside me at a desk in St Paul's School. I told him I was being hounded by a man of no account, though senior to myself. I told him I wanted to be left alone. He agreed with me.

'I will see to it,' he said, and so he did – that night.

General Montgomery drove up from his headquarters to lunch one day in the Western Desert with the 60th Kings Royal Rifles, who were bivouacked not far from 3rd RHA. I heard of his arrival, so I went over to see him. Instead of the usual driver, he liked one of his young offers from his HQ to drive his staff car. John Posten was one of these and rather a friend of mine, so while the general was having his lunch with the battalion officers, John and I lay in the scanty shade of the car and ate the most excellent lunch which had been provided for him; roast chicken it was. At length, Monty arrived, not best pleased with anyone, for he had felt it necessary to change the commanding officer, a very tough, though maybe unconventional, fighting officer, who was very highly thought of by his men. Seeing me, he said, 'What on earth are you doing here, Bob?' I told him that I had come over to see him. Slightly mollified, he said, 'I have no doubt you have eaten my lunch; now, come and tell me what the Germans are doing.' We parted amicably.

The next time I saw John Posten was at Antwerp. Monty had sent him up to see for himself how things were going. On his long way back, he was ambushed by a party of Germans, who killed him and his two companions, a very sad end to a brave man.

Chapter 17

SCHLESWIG-HOLSTEIN AND LUXEMBOURG

Admiral Dönitz, Hitler's nominated successor, was at his headquarters in Kiel at the time of the surrender. It was considered his reactions might be unpredictable.

I received a signal from army headquarters to proceed at once to Kiel, cross the bridge over the canal and report on conditions in Schleswig-Holstein. It was a lovely spring day, flowering lilacs everywhere, beautiful countryside, large herds of Friesian cattle, beautiful woods of beech trees, everything seemed quiet and peaceful. I left the regiment near the Kiel bridge – handy if I needed the guns, though I knew actual fighting was to be avoided if possible. I took only a small party with me and a young subaltern who was not much use. Leaving them in the yard of a most attractive farmhouse surrounded by a moat and with three enormous barns, I took my jeep to make a rapid survey of what was going on. All was quiet when I got back. I could not find the subaltern anywhere and was told he had gone off to investigate some shooting nearby.

The owner of the farm certainly did not look like a farmer; he was surly and definitely frightened out of his wits, especially when I told him I intended staying the night in his house. Not surprisingly, for when I opened the door of one of his barns there, sitting in the straw was the crew of a U-boat, all armed to the teeth. Their U-boat number 141 was settling down in the fiord nearby. I closed the doors again and walked over the plank bridge to the farmhouse to have a meal. In the dining room all seven officers of the U-boat were just sitting down to an excellent dinner when I opened the door and walked in. To say that they and I were astonished would be an understatement. I walked round the table collecting as many of their lugers as I could and left them to it, telling them that the owner of the farm would take them all to Kiel headquarters next morning and not to worry when my tank regiment pulled in during the night! It was certainly dicey and sleep was obviously out of the question, for they were a very tough lot.

In the morning I sent for the captain who was very young. I told him all his officers were free to move about the house but not to go across the plank bridge. We then went off to the fiord as I wanted to go over the U-boat. It had sunk pretty low and I hoped was now on the bottom, for I was determined to have a look inside. I was immensely interested. The crew lived in terribly congested conditions but the captain told me this was because some months back in the Atlantic they had picked up the crew of another U-boat which we had sunk.

He gave me the log, which showed they had been at sea for three months, and had sunk eighteen of our ships. This I sent to the Admiralty. They wrote saying that of the eighteen ships claimed as sunk, eight had limped home.

When we got back I found my subaltern dithering. He said one of the U-boat officers had come out, shot my sentry and disappeared. I told him what I thought of him for allowing this to happen, and was delighted to see the guns arriving along the road. I told the U-boat captain that I could not care less what happened to him, his officers or his crew and that he could march the lot to the German naval headquarters in Kiel, leaving behind every weapon they possessed. Quite a step it was to Kiel, maybe twenty miles. The apparently endless column of guns and tanks on the road was quite sufficient to take the stuffing out of the most belligerent of them.

All rather fun! Not many gunner COs have captured a U-boat and its crew. When I told Charles Armitage, my second-in-command, about it he obviously did not believe me, especially when he went down to the fiord where there was no sign of the U-boat as it was well and truly scuppered.

I told my three battery commanders to tour around and find pleasant houses or farms in which to billet themselves. My province extended from the Eckernförde in the north to the Kiel Canal in the south; it was pretty full already. Admiral Dönitz, Himmler and no doubt many others of such ilk were hidden round about.

I found for myself a charming newly-built house, called Lindhoff overlooking the Eckernförde, with a six hundred acre farm, worked by Poles and a very unpleasant German overseer. The house, on land taken from one of the Reventlow family, had been built by a certain Herr Löser, a bosom friend of Hitler from his early days. He was the first gauleiter of Poland, a war criminal of the first order. Hearing of my arrival, he took himself off in a large farm wagon, with his mistress plus baby, and disappeared. At the farm at the bottom of the hill, I found Löser's brother, his wife and two children; they had hanged themselves from a beam in the kitchen.

Quite a forthcoming Pole produced for my inspection a lovely white stallion, quiet and amiable. I rode him every morning. The Pole turned out to be an excellent groom. What a long time had passed since Betty and I had ridden out every morning in Cumberland! The weather was lovely, roe deer abounded; Riki the dachshund, an inveterate hunter, accompanied me everywhere. Life was really idyllic.

Then, of course, the usual problems arose. Germans and more Germans appeared. Several hundred wounded landed on the beach from somewhere or other.

The author, Lindhof

Lindhof

Riki

I found the village headmen quite excellent, sensible and co-operative. In no time at all, schools were converted into hospitals, every household for miles around produced blankets and every farm was ordered to produce the necessary food. All the labourers on the farms were Russian slave peasants. They now took to the woods, murdering anyone they came across after dark. They were a nuisance to everyone. Milk became a problem – hundreds of cows but no-one to milk them. Fortunately by chance I came across a large school, where fifty beautiful flaxen haired girls were being taught typewriting for the now defunct Luftwaffe. The place was run by a typical most unpleasing German frau. I sacked her on the spot, the girls then gleefully went off to the farms to learn how to milk cows. In one of the dormitories, there was a girl lying in bed, very frightened for some reason or other. I thought she had been whipped by that frau, so I ordered her up and I was glad to see that I had been mistaken.

Every day produced something new. At a small port, called Surrendorp, there were hundreds of two-men submarines. They would have been deadly had they been ready at the time of the invasion, each carried two torpedoes. I went out in the fiord in one of them. I did not care for it, or the young SS officer. He would have loved to see me drown. A little shack held a thousand pairs of U-boat commanders' night binoculars, excellently made but rather heavy. My sister watches the sea-birds feeding on the shore from her window in the Isle of Anglesey, with a pair I gave her.

The Reventlow family owned all the old big houses and most of the land. One branch of the family was very pro-British with English nannies, the other branch very pro-Nazi.

The order came that Himmler was to be found at all costs. A patrol of the Rifle Brigade picked up a Russian one evening with a note from Himmler to Doenitz. A trap was set and he was caught. I had given up searching for Löser, when he rang me up. He arrived saying that he was as good a man as Himmler and he would stand his trial. Both of them committed suicide in their cells – very unpleasant types.

One morning, Löser's secretary, rather an attractive girl, came to see me. She certainly was not a German, Swedish probably. She wanted to run the house for me, with the four Russian girls, whom I had sent down to the farm and a couple of Polish men.

If I had not had all my signallers, HQ staff, etc, it could have worked well, but I had to refuse her offer, whereupon she burst into tears! How nice it would have been if Renée Depage could have done all that but she was miles away with her Red Cross unit. I got word from her shortly after we had crossed the Rhine that they were moving up to take over a German Luftwaffe base to establish a medical transit camp to care for 34,000 Belgians who were serving forced labour, now streaming down the roads. After intense difficulty I found the place and she was delighted to see me. They had a first class mess, where I had an excellent dinner but the huts were very cold and damp. I left her my

Possibly the last photograph of Hitler 1945

sleeping bag, blankets and warm jerseys. I was amused to see that her very pretty girl-friend got all she wanted from my young driver, but no-one got anything at all from my Welsh batman!

The rest of the Armoured Brigade came up across the Kiel Canal, moving further north and west. They had several huge tiresome POW camps to look after, but marvellous duck shooting in the autumn. One morning, I was riding along the shore with my dachshund, when a beautiful yacht sailed up to my jetty. Eight German naval officers, who had sailed down from Norway approached, asking me to accept their surrender. They were very civil so I sent them into Kiel in a truck; I kept the yacht, with two excellent German seamen, for my officers. They were delighted with it and someone or other seemed to be out in the fiord every day.

People were continually visiting me to ask permission to cross the Kiel Canal. One of them, an elderly distinguished looking man, brought with him a mass of documents and diagrams. I could make nothing of them, so I sent the lot down to GHQ. Within a couple of days, a young staff captain arrived in an armoured car to fetch this man. Apparently he had been attached to Dachau Camp, where he experimented with great brutality on unfortunate women. He was one of the first of these inhuman monsters to hang.

My two Belgian hares loved the rich garden produce at Lindhoff. When I saw another family was imminent, I put them in the hen-house. They promptly disappeared underneath it, emerging later with ten delightful progeny.

A few days later, a party of army intelligence officers arrived. They had spent three days searching for Lindhoff. They demanded all the papers, which they said they knew I had, of the last meeting of the remaining heads of German states which had taken place on the day of the capitulation. Now I knew all about this and had searched most diligently inside and outside and had found nothing. However, as civility was not their strong line, I told them to contact their commanding officer on their wireless so that I could check their credentials. This took three hours, which drove them even more mad. I then told them I knew nothing of any state papers and that I was unable to read German. Unbelievably, within a couple of hours, they had found all the steel state boxes in the loose earth under the henhouse where my hares had made their burrow. This was an obvious place and I had never even thought of looking there!

My days passed very pleasantly. I was most comfortable. My study off the huge bedroom looked out over the woods and growing corn fields, where the roe deer roamed at will. I invited all the officers of the regiment to a dinner, a magnificent spread of venison, duck, lamb and suckling pig, marvellous vegetables and plentiful wine from the Lindhoff cellars, to which everyone did full justice, sleeping where they dined. I had a feeling that this life was too good to last and so it proved.

I received a signal from Major General Meade Dennis, Master Gunner, Royal Artillery, at Monty's headquarters, saying tersely that I had commanded a regiment of Horse Artillery for a long time and that it was time to give that honour to another colonel, who had been in England throughout the hostilities! I made no comment which provoked another signal offering me various alternatives. I again made no comment. I then received a slightly more conciliatory letter, suggesting that I might enjoy the leisure of being posted to Luxembourg as liaison officer to the Grand Duke and Grand Duchess. This I accepted, making my preparations to set off south in two weeks time. I must confess that as Luxembourg was within driving distance of Brussels, it did rather gild the lily I said goodbye to each battery in turn, then to General Roberts, who had arrived nearby, but Roscoe was too far away. The last thing I did was to order up my tank, and take down the pennant from the wireless mast; punctured and torn from bullets and splinters, it was in my racing colours – black with white cross-belts – and is hanging on the wall above me now. I remember having it made in Cairo.

Luxembourg, though a small country, is quite one of the most delightful in Europe. Well wooded, the Moselle winds its quiet way through the gentle slopes covered with vines, which produce excellent wines. Here I found the most delightful royal family: the Grand Duchess, stately and serene, was the head of state, her husband the Grand Duke a handsome middle-aged man, who had possessions in several countries in Europe, was constantly occupied in the after-war problems of his own country. The German occupation had not been pleasant for anyone. Their family, Prince Jean and his elegant sisters, were most welcoming and quite charming to me.

I found myself living in considerable comfort in company with an American military mission; what they did or where they did it I never discovered – a pleasant group of obviously very well-to-do citizens of the USA. The majority of them owned vast estates in the orange growing district. I was completely ignorant of their problems, so I played golf. The Grand Duke was busily bent on re-organising, re-equipping and retraining the royal guard of some two to three hundred young men. Here I helped him, flying over to England to consult the War Office in London, in obtaining what he required. I was also tied up with a British department in Brussels, which was especially pleasant for me, as I could visit Renée Depage, who had just returned with her Red Cross unit.

The city of Luxembourg is beautiful and the cathedral is quite lovely inside and out. I would have liked to learn more of its ancient history. My days passed very pleasantly. I attended several magnificent services in the cathedral, all of which were superbly conducted. The royal family could not have been kinder to a rather lonely British soldier, whose nerves were all too taut from the years of war. Many of the citizens invited me to long and simply prodigious dinners, each guest bringing the best of his wines, every bottle of which had to be consumed. In a few months, I was a different man. It was with great regret that I found my mission disbanded, myself and my dachshund being posted back to England.

Some years later, when Prince Jean was the Grand Duke, Queen Elizabeth conferred on him the highest honour in this land, Knight of the Garter. I could not have been more delighted.

21 ARMY GROUP

PERSONAL MESSAGE
FROM THE C-IN-C

(To be read out to all Troops)

1. On this day of victory in Europe I feel I would like to speak to all who have served and fought with me during the last few years. What I have to say is very simple, and quite short.

2. I would ask you all to remember those of our comrades who fell in the struggle. They gave their lives that others might have freedom, and no man can do more than that. I believe that He would say to each one of them:

    "Well done, thou good and faithful servant."

3. And we who remain have seen the thing through to the end; we all have a feeling of great joy and thankfulness that we have been preserved to see this day.

    We must remember to give the praise and thankfulness where it is due:

    "This is the Lord's doing, and it is marvellous in our eyes."

4. In the early days of this war the British Empire stood alone against the combined might of the axis powers. And during those days we suffered some great disasters; but we stood firm: on the defensive, but striking blows where we could. Later we were joined by Russia and America; and from then onwards the end was in no doubt. Let us never forget what we owe to our Russian and American allies; this great allied team has achieved much in war; may it achieve even more in peace.

5. Without doubt, great problems lie ahead; the world will not recover quickly from the upheaval that has taken place; there is much work for each one of us.

    I would say that we must face up to that work with the same fortitude that we faced up to the worst days of this war. It may be that some difficult times lie ahead for our country, and for each one of us personally. If it happens thus, then our discipline will pull us through; but we must remember that the best discipline implies the subordination of self for the benefit of the community.

6. It has been a privilege and an honour to command this great British Empire team in western Europe. Few commanders can have had such loyal service as you have given me. I thank each one of you from the bottom of my heart.

7. And so let us embark on what lies ahead full of joy and optimism. We have won the German war. Let us now win the peace.

8. Good luck to you all, wherever you may be.

B. L. Montgomery

Germany,
May, 1945.

Field-Marshal,
C.-in-C.,
21 Army Group.

HONOURS AND AWARDS

to officers and other ranks
of the 13th Regiment Honourable Artillery Company
Royal Horse Artillery
during the campaign from Normandy to Lübeck 1944-1945

Officers:

Distinguished Service Order	2
Military Cross	8
Mention in Despatches	11
C-in-C Certificates	1
American Award – Silver Star	1

Other Ranks:

Military Cross	1
Military Medals	9
Mention in Despatches	10
C-in-C Certificates	16

Poscript

After the war, and his brief sojourn in Luxembourg, Bob Daniell returned to England and was given command of a regiment of anti-aircraft gunners in East Anglia. In 1947 he was promoted to Brigadier and moved to Shoeburyness, which he described as the prize station of the coastal defence gunners.

In 1951 he was invited to apply for membership of the Honourable Corps of Gentlemen at Arms, which entailed his retiring from the regular army. A quote from his diary:

"I had had many years of most pleasant service and was indeed honoured to accept this invitation. The Corps of Gentlemen at Arms has the most delightful mess in St James's Palace, founded in 1509. This small body of twenty-seven gentlemen and four officers, all distinguished retired officers, have been ever since that date, and still are today, the sovereign's closest guard. They are *ipso facto* members of the Royal Household, and attend the sovereign at all state functions. I had twenty years most enjoyable service with many memorable occasions, such as the lying in state of His Majesty King George VI and of Her Majesty Queen Mary, the Coronation, several Royal weddings and innumerable state functions, including all visits of foreign heads of state. At length in 1971, by which time I was the senior gentleman, I had to retire, having actively served the sovereign for fifty-two years."

Bob and Betty Daniell settled in Hessett in Suffolk in the early nineteen fifties, and subsequently moved close by to Tostock, where they remained until they died, Betty in January 1994 and Bob in December 1996. They were married for sixty-five years.

These memoirs were dictated in 1983, but not published until 1998.

Brigadier Daniell was awarded the following honours:

Distinguished Service Order
Bar to Distinguished Service Order
Palestine Medal 1939
Four Campaign Medals – 8th Army Bar
Twice mentioned in despatches for
    bravery in battle, 1939-45
Commandant de l'Ordre de Mérite
    d'Adolphe de Nassau
Chevalier de l'Ordre de Léopold I avec Palme
Croix de Guerre de Belgique avec Palme
Member of Honourable Corps of
    Gentlemen at Arms 1951-1971

Honourable Corps of Gentlemen at Arms

The author, Gentleman at Arms